'A knockout read about how one woman finds her voice in the face of gurus, religion and her own fears, *The Serpent Rising* is an honest account that's as eye-watering as it is inspiring. The penultimate moments had me cheering out loud.'

—Michael Burge, author of *Tank Water* and director of the High Country Writers Festival.

The Serpent Rising

A Journey of Spiritual Seduction

Mary Garden

JUSTITIA BOOKS

JUSTITIA BOOKS

First published in Australia in 1988
by Brolga Publishing, Brisbane

A revised edition published in 2003
by Sid Harta Publishers, Victoria, Australia

This edition published by Justitia Books
PO Box 306, Chewton 3451 Victoria

Copyright © Mary Garden, 2023

The right of Mary Garden to be identified as the Author of the Work has been asserted in accordance with the Copyright, Designs and Patents Act 1988.

All rights reserved. No part of this publication may be reproduced, stored in a retrieval system, or transmitted, in any form or by any means, electronic, mechanical, photocopying, recording or otherwise, without the prior written permission of the publisher.

A catalogue record for this book is available from the National Library of Australia

ISBN: 978-0-646896-98-4

Typesetting: Chameleon Print Design
Cover: Immaculate Studios, Pakistan
Cover illustration: Parvati Offers Bhang to Shiva
Photograph on back cover: Mary Garden having an 'Energy Darshan' with Rajneesh (Osho), Poona, India, November 1979

Mary Garden was born in Whakatane, New Zealand, and grew up in the coastal town of Tauranga. She trained to be a teacher at Hamilton Teachers College, and in 1970 she obtained a B. Ed. from Waikato University.

After her Indian odyssey, she settled in Australia and now lives in the historic Goldfields town of Chewton, in regional Victoria.

Mary became a freelance journalist in 2003 and her work has appeared in a range of publications in various countries, including Australia, New Zealand, the UK and America. In 2014, she received a PhD in journalism from the University of the Sunshine Coast; her study was on journalists' use of blogs and Twitter.

Mary's collection of poems *Coming Together: a journey through passion* was published in 1992. Her biography *Sundowner of the Skies: the story of Oscar Garden, the forgotten aviator* was published in 2019 by New Holland and was short-listed for the NSW Premier's History Award 2020 for a book of international significance.

The Serpent Rising: a journey of spiritual seduction has had enduring appeal and several editions have been published over the years. It won the High Country Indie Book Award 2021.

www.marygarden.com.au

For Natalya and Eamon

Author's Note

This book is based on my experiences in India in the 1970s. It was first self-published in 1988, when I wrote the story as a work of fiction, and called the main character Helena Pearson. Regardless, readers and reviewers read it as a memoir. In 2003, I revised and republished the book as a memoir, with an updated epilogue.

What was thought to be a passing fad of the 1960s and 1970s has not disappeared. People still surrender their minds and bodies to gurus and yoga teachers, even those who have been exposed as frauds, charlatans and abusers.

Recently, there has been renewed interest in my book, especially with the documentaries *Wild Wild Country* (Rajneesh/Osho), *Bikram: Yogi, Guru, Predator* (Bikram Choudhury) and *The Vow* (Keith Ranierre/NXIVM). The #MeToo movement has exposed countless men guilty of sexual harassment and assault. Now #MeToo is shaking the yoga world and gurus who claim to be enlightened.

As with the earlier editions, the names of some of the people I met have been changed to protect the privacy of these individuals.

Mary Garden
2023

Mary Garden in 1973, the day she left for India

x

Kedarnath, Uttarakhand, 1978.

Facing page: doing yoga, Auckland, 1976

*At Puttaparthi,
Andhra Pradesh,
May 1973.*

Above: Premvarni with five of his disciples in 1975; I am 3rd from the left.

Left: Balyogi Premvarni meditating on the roof of his ashram at Rishikesh, 1973.

Religion claims to be in possession of an absolute truth; but its history is a history of errors and heresies. It gives us the promise and prospect of a transcendent world — far beyond the limits of our human experience — and it remains human, all too human.

Ernst Cassier
An Essay on Man

Chapter 1

Learning to Fly

I t all began with a notice in the window of a health-food shop in Queen Street, Auckland, back at the beginning of the year 1973. I usually ignored such pieces of paper that had begun to decorate odd shops with increasing frequency in recent years, but there was a picture of a snake that caught my attention. Even though I usually recoiled from images of such creatures (there are no snakes in New Zealand), this one was different.

This snake was coiled upwards with its forked tongue reaching as if for the sky instead of slinking and sliding low through dark places on the ground. Bordering the notice were intricate hand-drawings of pink lotus flowers, the stems of which were entwined and the petals wide opened.

I found myself reading the words sprinkled below this strange picture. There was going to be a celebration that night at a place called the Henderson Yoga Ashram. This would be led by an Indian swami (a Hindu religious teacher) and evidently the first swami to ever visit New Zealand. I had heard of this so-called ashram or Hindu 'spiritual community', as there were rumours around the university that hippies who took drugs and practised black magic visited and sometimes stayed there.

I cringed at the thought of Eastern brands of religion being imported into this country. Even though I sometimes practised yoga exercises, (but only for their physical benefits), the Hindu religion along with all other religions seemed to me to be mere escapism. They were for people who were too frightened to believe in a Godless existence — a life where we are born and where we die. For years I had tried to believe that death was simply a return to the dust of the earth, not a doorway to heaven or hell or some kind of rebirth.

But all the way back to my flat in the outskirts of Auckland, and on and off during the day, I kept remembering the notice and the picture of that upward-reaching, coiled snake. Although I had no desire to attend some weird religious ceremony, a strong almost compulsive feeling that I should kept arising in me. I wondered whether it was just curiosity but there was also the fear that perhaps, subconsciously, I wanted to seek some kind of religious solace. And why had I been so fascinated by that snake and the pink lotus flowers?

When I was young I had been a Christian believer and as a child had often dreamt of being a missionary or nun when I grew up. As a child I believed everything I was taught in the church my father made us attend each Sunday. There we were told that God would punish us when we did wrong and would reward and bless us when we were good. There seemed to be clear divisions then of what constituted heaven and hell, good and evil: they were all stated in the Bible. As well as believing in a kind, benevolent father-figure way up in the heavens above the skies watching over me all the time, I also believed in guardian angels who were supposed to (and I imagined they did) come near me to comfort me during times of sadness.

However, as years passed I realised it wasn't so simple. There were times at school and at home when I was punished for doing no wrong and there were times when I got away with misdemeanours. Was this the working of a just and omnipotent God? And why were church services so boring? As I questioned the teaching and practices of Presbyterian Christianity, I became more and more confused until doubt finally eroded my childhood faith. I stopped going to church and Sunday school. I stopped praying to God and the angels at night before drifting off to sleep. And even stopped calling out for help to Jesus. Instead I pasted pictures of Elvis all over the ceiling of my bedroom and had him watching over me instead.

Adoration of Elvis and then the Beatles ushered me into the sixties, and by the time I was sixteen — my first year at university — life was a constant round of sex, alcohol, parties and sometimes experimenting with drugs. Many of us smoked pot and we sometimes smoked it with lecturers at parties, and most of us tried other drugs such as LSD. I don't remember anyone warning us of the dangers, except the possibility of a police raid. We believed we were somehow part of a massive movement that would bring peace to earth. Then we would no longer have to worry about America or Russia putting their finger on the button of the 'big one' — the phrase used for the atomic bomb that would destroy the planet earth. We mocked our parents and called them square. Even though we were into the notion of 'free love' (loving each other and sleeping with anyone we felt like) I still found myself with the romantic notion of wanting to fall in love with only one man, the love of my life. Such idealism was still featured in the romantic paperbacks and films of that time and I longed to fall madly in love and remain in love for the rest of my life. But none of the relationships I had (mostly with older men) lasted.

But after seeing that notice at the health-food shop, I was not thinking of romance or dreaming of 'the perfect man'. Instead I kept thinking of the notice and its snake and pink flowers. For the rest of the day I tried to resist this pull, this attraction to attend the Hindu ceremony until finally, towards evening, I suddenly decided to go. Within minutes I had changed into a brightly coloured floral skirt and a large striped men's shirt that was left hanging down over the skirt rather than tucking it into my waistband. I raced outside, leapt into my little grey Morris Minor, and headed out towards the Waitakere Ranges that fringe the Western reaches of Auckland. As I drove I could feel a depressing sadness permeating me like thick, suffocating smog. I had often felt like this during the past year, which had been the most harrowing of my life in spite of continued academic success.

In five years I had already collected a degree, a teaching diploma and a sizeable wad of research manuscript towards a Masters degree; the further possibility of a future job as a lecturer had already been mentioned. But this success was overshadowed by other things.

In the past year my closest girlfriend had made several suicide attempts. I felt helpless and guilty because I did not know how to help her. My mother, whom I had always been close to and able to confide in even about intimate things, had become distant. Perhaps she was menopausal, retreating somewhere inside herself in lost and passing dreams? I did not know how to reach her. I also discovered that a boyfriend, a lecturer in Physics, was secretly fascinated by the occult and by Hitler and that leader's rise to power. Days after this discovery he was badly burnt by a hand-made bomb that had accidentally exploded; he survived, just. Our relationship did not. I felt mortified that I had become involved with such a person and never was aware that he was making such things. By the end of the year I was beginning to feel completely inadequate in relating to people. Was there something wrong with me that was causing these unfolding dramas?

It was dark when I pulled up outside the ashram in the outskirts of the small town of Henderson. Realising that the ceremony would have probably started, I sat in my car for a few minutes feeling ill at ease, wondering whether to turn around and go back to Auckland. But I finally dragged myself out and walked up the path edged on both sides by foot-high grass. Long sticky paspalum grass kept wrapping themselves around my lower calves and left their seeds in sticky blobs on my skin.

The ashram was a dilapidated wooden two-storied house surrounded by towering trees whose branches leaned and crept against its walls. The place looked in darkness yet there was a long line of cars parked down the road outside the entrance. The only noises that could be heard were the hum of the traffic on the distant motorway, crickets shrieking in their monotonous tone and frogs croaking to each other. Up in the night sky a moon was lying on its back as it floated above the clouds.

Upon reaching the wooden steps I noticed they were covered by untidy mounds of shoes and sandals. I kicked off my sandals, tiptoed inside the house and made my way towards a room from which came a faint glow of light and some strange murmuring sounds. Nervously I peeked around the door.

A few candles provided the only light at one end

of the room, large vases of flowers were placed at all corners and there were long garlands of flowers hanging around various pictures on the wall. The smell of sweet incense filled the air and thin threads of smoke were dancing in whirls and spirals upwards. A group of people sat cross-legged on the floor, their attention fixed on a figure at the far end of the room. I slipped quietly inside and found a place to sit at the back of the group, next to one of the sidewalls.

The swami was a large man, naked from the waist upward. What looked like an orange sheet was draped awkwardly around the lower portion of his body and left to dangle unevenly over the floor. His head was closely shaven and his brown skin was shiny almost glowing in the dark. I noticed his enormous stomach protruding over the top of the garment. The swami turned to face the altar — a sideboard covered with a white cloth — on which were placed various pictures, brass incense holders and candles, flowers and fruit. He began to chant some peculiar sounds, deep sounds that appeared to be coming from his belly and echoing upwards and outwards. I sat there, watching him as he chanted and waved a brass lamp slowly in large circles around an ornate picture of one of the Hindu deities.

I had never looked closely at one of these pictures before as they always seemed grotesque, even sinister, with their multiple heads and arms. This particular picture, which was well illuminated by the candles alongside it, was a figure with only one head and one set of arms though in other ways it appeared unworldly, hardly human. The god was sitting in full lotus position in the snow with his back erect and his head held high. Long matted hair fell over his shoulders, his face was smooth with no sign of facial hair, numerous snakes were entwined around his neck and upper body and a third eye gleamed from his forehead. Placed at his feet was a strange black object that looked like an erect penis embedded in two lips, resting on a curved base. These slippery looking snakes and this phallic object reminded me of some terrifying nightmares I could remember clearly from my childhood.

These dreams occurred when I was about six years old. I can remember the small room I slept in and shared with my younger sister. I did not like that room. The wallpaper was ugly, with large brown-yellow flowers splattered over it. It was so ugly our parents did not mind that we drew all over it with our crayons and sometimes tore strips off it. I can still remember this wallpaper vividly because in these dreams monsters slid slowly down the wallpaper until they crawled on top of me in my narrow bed. They were like sirens. Attractive from a distance with long blond hair and sweet smiles but as they loomed closer, I noticed their eye-teeth, horns sticking from their heads and blazing yellow-red eyes. They made screeching and snarling sounds as they crawled over me and their slippery hands slid up and down my legs and played in between them. I would lie there without moving. These recurring dreams seemed so real that when I finally struggled free from them, my fear persisted. I used to think that God had sent the Devil to punish me for something dreadful I had done. I had no idea what it could be.

In the dreams the name for these creatures that enjoyed tormenting me was cannas. Some years later I was to discover that the nickname the kids in my neighbourhood used for penis was canna or lily. Yet I did not remember making any connection at the time with these nightmares. Thirty years later my younger sister told me that the neighbour next door took us into his hen house covered with vines and forced us to have oral sex with him. She said she loved it but I had run screaming down the long dusty driveway back towards our house. She claims she had done this more than once, but that I never went back. About that time though, I vaguely remember pulling off the head and limbs of my favourite doll and burying them underneath the tall pine trees outside my bedroom window. Of the hen house and oral sex I have no memory. A few years before my mother finally said she could remember me running down the driveway and telling her (and my father) what had happened even though whenever I had tried to discuss it previously she would say 'Oh, you've got such a good imagination'.

Shuddering at these memories, as I gazed at the picture behind the swami, other memories also began to surface — vague memories (or were they mere imaginings?) that I could not connect to anything in this lifetime. There was this feeling that I already knew the symbolism behind these snakes wrapped around the god's bare torso and this black phallic-shaped object. And there was a sense of closeness, almost a familiarity, with this god Shiva whose opened third eye was shining like a diamond in the centre of his forehead, an eye with a calm and an all-knowing quality. In some strange way this eye looked real as if it was meant to be there, seeing all, in contrast to the two eyes that were almost closed.

I began to feel mesmerised, as if my consciousness was being sucked into this picture. At the same time, the words the swami was chanting were passing through my brain, soothing tension and they seemed to be slowing my thoughts down, even stopping them completely at times. I closed my eyes and sighed. The swami's words seemed familiar though I did not know what they meant. My attention then went to my heart region because a warmth was there, getting stronger until it felt as if I was pouring out love. I felt in love but with no one in particular. Being in love I was giving out love to all round me. I had never felt anything like this in my life. Beads of sweat covered my forehead and were sliding down my face, which felt delicate and soft and no longer tight and strained. An extraordinary sense of the deepest peace was seeping through me. A peace that grew into ecstasy itself. The thought occurred to me that I had been hypnotised by perhaps the swami or even some power in the picture of Shiva, but I didn't care. Whatever it was that I was feeling I wanted more.

How long I sat there like that I do not know, but when I finally opened my eyes people were beginning to get up and move about. I slowly stood up and walked out without saying a word to anyone. Reaching the front steps, I noticed the moon was floating through a clear space now, the clouds having vanished from sight. The cool night air washed over my face and as I walked down the path towards my car, I noticed my whole body had a new gracefulness and lightness about it. The heaviness of my negative feelings had lifted. Now I was bathing in sublime peace.

I decided to leave university and go to India as soon as possible. I would go and learn more about this Hindu religion. This land of India, this pearly tear on the cheek of Asia, had begun to possess me. I had no doubt I had found what I had been looking for all my life.

For the next week, I visited the Henderson Yoga Ashram every day and stayed for some hours most nights. I had to drag myself away when it was time to go for I felt completely at home there and also felt very much at ease with the four other young people who lived there. At the end of the week I was given permission by the owner of the ashram, a man called Mr Postleweight but known as 'Guruji', to go and live there. Guruji was an elderly man in his late seventies. He was incredibly energetic and seemed to be in excellent health. He spent most of his time practising, teaching, and preaching a branch of yoga called 'hatha yoga'. This branch of yoga includes *asanas* (physical postures), *pranayama* (breathing exercises) and *kriyas* (techniques to purify the body including short fasts). Guruji had the appearance of an Indian ascetic, with his lean body, his white hair falling well past his shoulders and a long raggedy moustache and beard. His clothes were simple, baggy, usually white in colour, and he often wore just sandals or else went barefooted. Most of his teeth were missing, except for a few crooked ones in the front and his nose was large and bulbous. He smiled a lot (especially when talking about yoga) but at other times he seemed rather distracted perhaps from the effect of holding various yoga *asanas* for long periods of time or from the many ventures he was involved with. He had a dream that he could spread yoga throughout New Zealand, humanise and uplift what he called a spiritually derelict society. He was often away from the ashram giving lectures and demonstrations around Auckland or he would shut himself up in his room spending many hours writing articles for magazines and letters to newspapers.

We paid Guruji a moderate amount of money for food and accommodation. Most of the vegetables we ate came from the ashram gardens in which we worked daily for as long as we wished. There was little routine to life in this ashram, the only rules being no smoking, drugs, or Western music. Guruji led a morning hatha yoga class and in the evenings we all sat together to chant and meditate. These nightly sessions I found intoxicating. We would light incense and candles, sit in a circle and hold hands to pass on the energy, and chant Hindu *mantras* over and over.

The sounds of these *mantras* would resonate in different parts of my body especially at the top of my head, in my forehead, just above my eyebrows and in the region of my heart. I would feel energy moving, sometimes heat, and often a sensation as if these areas were opening up. I was convinced I was connected to some higher energy, some powerful force, and that this force was God. I had never before felt so happy or at peace with myself.

At the ashram I slept on a mattress on the floor in one of the rooms on the upper-storey of the large rambling house. I even set up my own *puja* (worship) place with two framed pictures — one of Shiva, the other of Krishna. Around the pictures I arranged trinkets, flowers, incense and candles. I became a vegetarian and started various purifications, such as fasting and colonic irrigation, to cleanse my digestive system.

Guruji gave me many books to read — mainly autobiographies — including Paramahansa Yogananda's *Autobiography of a Yogi*, Paul Brunton's *Search for Secret India*, and the books of Herman Hesse. My favourite was *Siddhartha* by Herman Hesse, and I hoped one day I too would sit by a great river, realise all the mysteries of the universe and discover my true nature. Each day was an adventure as I discovered all these ways of progressing along the road to 'enlightenment'. And the greatest realisation of all was that I no longer needed to worry about men, searching or waiting for romance, looking for the ideal man to marry and live happily ever after with. I was in love with God and would not have to worry about that relationship ending.

Since the night of my conversion I was a different person. I believed that now I was spiritual and I wanted little to do with those who weren't. Those moods of depression and loneliness had mysteriously vanished and in their place were tremendous joy and calmness. I felt like someone who had lived an unfulfilling life on the bottom storey of a multi-storeyed building, completely unaware there were people living on the storeys above me who all shared something in common — they were consumed by the quest for spiritual development. It was a revelation. How had I missed all this going on behind my back?

During the next two weeks I left university, burnt my half-finished Masters thesis, gave away tea-chests full of university texts and other books and also gave away most of my possessions. I sold some of the larger things such as my sewing machine and car, and also cashed in the BHP shares my grandmother had given me for my twenty-first birthday. Preparations were made to go to India and I purchased a plane ticket to Delhi. Guruji was keen for me to go to Rishikesh, in the Himalayas, where the headquarters of the Divine Life Movement (founded by Swami Shivananda), was situated. The Henderson Yoga Ashram was a branch of this organization formed to propagate and spread yoga in the traditional way. Although my mother had already arranged for me to get a British passport several years before, on account of my father being a British citizen, I now went and obtained a New Zealand passport so that I could have a spare one.

A week before I was due to fly to India, the ashram residents were invited to a vegetarian feast at the house of some fellow seekers who were Sathya Sai Baba devotees. Guruji didn't go. He said this group was just a cult and their leader a black magician. But Margaret and Robert, who had been at the ashram for over a year, told me not to take any notice of Guruji. They said he had a closed mind and was not open to other spiritual paths. They however believed in 'the brotherhood' — any person or groups who were on the road to 'enlightenment' were friends of theirs.

A medical practitioner, Stanley Roberts, had just returned from the ashram of Sai Baba in south India. During the meal we listened to him proclaim that Sai Baba was an *avatar*, an incarnation of God and the most extraordinary person on this planet. Stanley was sitting opposite me and soon I noticed he was paying particular attention to me. He was a quite unattractive man. He was short; his blond straight hair was unfashionably short and plastered back over his large elfin ears. But there was something different about Stanley; his eyes captivated me for they were large, blue and very clear, almost luminous. With those remarkable eyes he mesmerised me. At times I glanced over at Margaret and Robert and was surprised to see looks of indifference, almost boredom, on their faces. They continued to sit there, saying nothing. The few other devotees who lived in the house sat with us and looked absorbed in what Stanley was saying, even though they would have heard it before.

That night I listened to wondrous tales of Baba healing the sick, curing the lame, transforming himself into other forms and identities and transporting himself great distances and performing miracles. Stanley told us how Baba could materialise objects such as necklaces, bracelets and rings from thin air. Daily he materialised a sacred ash called *vibhuti* from the palm of his hand and passed this out to 'deserving' devotees. I sat there and listened and believed everything Stanley said. His eyes were radiant. His devotion to Baba was total. His enthusiasm catching. I caught it: Sai Baba fever. My mind boggled at the possibility of a being with such powers on earth at this time. I was filled with awe. Was it Sai Baba who was behind all those strange and remarkable changes in my life? I would go to him. Surrender my life to him.

The next morning, I went and changed my plane ticket. I decided not to go to Delhi and then up to Rishikesh. Instead I would fly to Madras and then across to Bangalore. I would go to Sai Baba.

A few days before I was due to leave, I travelled down to the home of my parents at Tauranga in the Bay of Plenty. When I announced that I was going to India my father screwed up his thin crinkled face. 'You're stark, staring mad. It all sounds like a lot of baloney. You'll catch some disease and die. It's a filthy place.'

I pointed out that he had been to India several times during his pioneer aviation days in the early 1930s and he had made that almost suicidal trip in his Gypsy Moth from England to Australia with insufficient water or food and with hastily copied maps. He snorted and shuffled off to the glasshouse muttering, 'You're absolutely bonkers. Don't know what the young people are coming to today. They want everything. They should have lived through the Depression.'

My father had been a market gardener since he had married. But he had a past before that, which I had seldom heard about while growing up. It took many years for me to learn that my father was the fourth aviator to fly solo from England to Australia. What made his trip remarkable was that he was a novice pilot with only 40 hours of flying experience. And the sole purpose of his flight, in a second-hand plane, was not to break any flying records but to accumulate enough hours to obtain his commercial flying licence! The Australians called him the 'Sundowner of the Skies' because he appeared and disappeared on their land unannounced, unheralded — a mystery airman. He had also played a major role in commercial aviation, but had left suddenly in the early forties after a disagreement with TEAL (Tasman Empire Airways Ltd) over its future direction and policy especially the purchase of the Sandringham flying boats. I had even read in one magazine that it was my father who had laid the foundations on which TEAL and Air New Zealand had built a reputation for flight safety and operational proficiency renowned amongst airlines. Perhaps the full story of his days in both pioneering and commercial aviation will never be told. He seldom spoke of it when we were growing up and he refused to talk to any of the reporters or journalists who occasionally walked unannounced up the long driveway to our secluded house.

I watched him shuffle away, his baggy khaki trousers stained green and yellow from his precious tomato plants ballooning out from his thin body. For as long as I could remember he had always worked long hours, seven days a week, and my mother had always worked with him. When we were young, my brother, sister and I usually had to keep out of their way and much of our time out of school was spent exploring the beaches, the cliffs and the countryside near our house. We enjoyed being away from our father because he was usually very strict and extremely critical of the way we did things or carried out tasks. Our mother, in contrast, was almost always patient, understanding and gentle as if she was trying to over-compensate for his harshness.

As I grew up, I regarded my father as narrow-minded, conservative, dogmatic, old-fashioned, and a fundamentalist in his religious views. My mother, reared in Roman Catholicism, seemed to be broad-minded, accommodating and liberated. As a teenager I was proud of my mother and embarrassed by my father. Looking back, my teenage years seemed to have been a revolt against his moralistic beliefs and an embrace of the freedom and liberation my mother's viewpoint offered. But now, after finding God again, I knew that the answer did not lie in worldly living, or in the humanistic ideals prized by my mother. Five years of being free to do my own thing, to follow my desires and urges had only reaped hangovers and depression. Five years of academic study had also led to disillusionment for there seemed to be no absolute truth in science or philosophy — only ideas that change and results that change according to manipulable variables of research.

Thankfully, I had been saved from the perils of materialism and intellectualism. Now for the first time in my life everything seemed clear because of the revelation that God was the answer to my problems and that this God could only be found through Eastern mysticism. Not only did Hinduism seem to embrace the Christianity of my youth but also I had been told and had read in various books at the ashram that the teachings of the Bible had been distorted over the centuries. I learned that Christ was another label for *avatar*. Jesus, Buddha and Sai Baba were all *avatars*, incarnations of God. The notion of self-realisation came evidently from the biblical principle: 'the kingdom of heaven lies within you'. I also read that during his life, Jesus even travelled to India in order to study and practise yoga in the Himalayas and that this training accounted for his miracles and his powers of healing. I was disappointed that my father could not see the truth. Why didn't he see that Sai Baba was another Christ?

Watching my father walk away to the glasshouse, I felt anguish because I could not reach him, because we had never been close. Now I wished that as a child I could have found a way to warm and open his heart, to sit on his knee and for him to tell stories to me. But nothing could change my mind about going to India. My father had made a decision to make his epic flight in 1930 and had gone ahead with little thought or planning: it seemed to be the only thing of significance that he had done in his life. Well, for the first time in my life I too had found something that had truly captured my heart and nothing was going to stop me pursuing it. I had no desire to be trapped in the cage of domesticity. I wanted to be an adventurer following my father's footsteps, but I didn't want to explore the skies. I wanted to explore the inner world — the sky space of the mind and the oceans of the heart. Now I could feel a part of him in me and I didn't hate that part. I treasured it.

My mother also was not happy about my plans, but she was as much worried about the psychological dangers as she was about the physical risks. 'This Sai Baba character sounds rather strange. I hope you're not getting caught up in some weird cult? Now you just be careful there.'

Attempts to reassure her with stories of Sai Baba's professed powers and status only made her even more concerned. So I changed the subject and began to think what I needed to take on the journey. The fewer things the better.

The next day my mother drove me back to Auckland to the airport. There was rain falling in steady sheets from a drab, grey sky. As I sat there I thought how much it rained in this country. I sighed as I fingered the sandalwood beads around my neck. My mother glanced over at me. 'I don't know what's got into you. You're not like my daughter anymore. Not the Mary you used to be. I hope you know what you're doing rushing away like this. Turning your back on your teaching career and all the study you've done.'

I groaned, hugged my knees up to my chest, and

began to rock backwards and forwards as I stared through the windscreen at the rain streaking. Finally I said, 'I'm happy for the first time in my life, Mum. There's some meaning in my life at last. I know exactly where I'm going and what I want. I can't wait to be in India, sitting at Baba's feet.'

Turning my head, I saw a grimace on my mother's drawn face but she said, 'As long as you are happy, dear. That's all that matters.' I had heard that phrase countless times from her throughout my life. It always annoyed me.

When we reached the terminal building, I lifted out my half-empty backpack, which mainly contained my sleeping bag. All my worldly possessions in one backpack. My mother then said: 'That dress you've got on, dear. Are you sure it's suitable?' Before I had time to answer, she said, 'Don't you have any other shoes than those rubber sandals you flap around in?'

I was wearing a loose, white crimplene kaftan (with slits up to the knees), which I had roughly sewn up myself. I didn't feel like replying to my mother's questions, but I knew she was trying hard to understand this 'trip' I was on. I explained that white was the colour of purity and surely she didn't want me to wear stiletto heels to India. I was going to live the life of a Hindu nun. However, realising I might never see her again I made an effort to be civil and reassured her that as soon as I got to India, I would buy some more suitable clothes there.

One hour later I caught another glimpse of my mother. But this time she was far away. She was waving hesitantly as she leant over the rails of the observation deck. The plane was beginning to move down the runway. The rain had eased now, but there was still a greyness veiling the sunlight. I waved back although it probably was impossible for her to see me at that distance against the moving blur of the aircraft. I knew I was disappointing her. She had wanted to live her unfulfilled dreams through me. I had always been the one she didn't have to worry about, the one she could rely on. But I had often felt so miserable, even tormented, and had just put on a happy mask. However, becoming 'spiritual' had given me the confidence to break away from my divided personality with ease, or so it seemed. Now I felt whole and had no difficulty showing to the world my newfound purity, piety and child-like joy. It was as if I was beginning a new life as a different person, a much happier and freer person. If I ever did come back from India it would be to spiritually enlighten my parents and save them from the perils and miseries of worldly life.

Although I was finally leaving, it didn't feel like I was running away. Instead it felt like I was learning to fly. I had run away so often as a child but I always returned after an hour or two and nothing had changed. When my father was angry with me, I would run away and hide in our secret crumbling caves in the cliffs. Or I would climb up and nestle in gnarled branches of high trees that seemed to disappear into the sky. Sometimes I'd run down to the beach below and lie on its soft white sand and listen to the gentle waves reaching for the shore.

Apart from those dreadful nightmares about cannas, the only other dreams I remember having as a child were dreams of running away. Those dreams where you ran and ran and never got anywhere, never reached safety and where often there was the feeling of being pursued. I remember my mother and my two aunts saying that I was always running. They used to laugh and say, 'Our Mary — always rushing. That girl will get anything she wants. You'd think she was out to conquer the world.' My mother often told the story that in fact I had been rushing even before I was born. As the story goes (how true it is I don't know), my mother, heavily pregnant, fell off the back of the truck where she had been loading boxes of tomatoes. By the time she had reached the hospital at Whakatane and was assigned a bed, I rushed out of my mother's womb, wasting no time in drawn-out labour.

But I didn't have to rush or run away anymore. God was taking care of me now. He was flying me to his only incarnation on earth at this time. As the plane picked up speed, I turned away from the window and realised that I was grinning. The lady next to me was wiping her eyes with a lacy handkerchief. But I didn't feel sad. I felt excited and happy and didn't care if I never saw New Zealand again. I didn't feel as though I belonged to that country anymore. In fact I don't think I ever felt as if I had truly belonged there.

The plane wrenched itself upwards. Soon we were sailing through soft white clouds, climbing far away from those two small islands stuck down there in that lonely corner of the world. I decided to stop dwelling on my past. Surely that chapter was closed now — dead and absorbed into a new beginning. I glanced across at the lady sitting next to me.

She had taken out her make-up bag and was peering into the small mirror of her compact. When I turned away I could still see her in my peripheral vision and watched her begin to fill in the cracks on her face with thick, pasty foundation. She then patted soft powder over the top. Watching this I realised how lucky I was that the vanity game was now over for me. All that time I used to waste putting on and cleaning off make-up.

I glanced down at the book I was clutching on my lap. My talisman of protection. On the cover was the strange face of Sai Baba, which was surrounded by the black frizzy hair that his devotees likened to a halo. My heart pounding, I turned away to gaze at the smooth empty sky outside. Soon I would see him.

Chapter 2

It's All His Grace

The long flight to India, with an eight-hour stopover in Singapore, was neither tedious nor tiring as my mind was at peace with only one train of thought — Sai Baba and blissful fantasies of what may lie ahead.

I arrived at Madras airport in the middle of a summer night. As I stood at the door of the aeroplane ready to disembark the heat engulfed me, filling my mouth and nostrils. A slight breeze brought no relief but just fanned the heat. It was different from anything I had experienced but I breathed deeply into it and welcomed it: the heat of India. And standing there looking out I had the feeling of having been here before, that India was a country I already knew intimately.

As I walked down the steps and across to the terminus, which resembled several wooden barns huddled together, everyone I glanced at smiled or grinned at me. Tears came to my eyes as I smiled back, because for the first time in my life this felt like home. I felt one of them, although I was the only European in sight. I was enchanted by the way they looked and the way they dressed, the darkness of their skins, their black sparkling eyes, the graceful flowing garments of the women, the loose pajamas that the majority of the men were wearing. Many of them laughed loudly, smiled broadly and none of them seemed to be in any great hurry to get to the terminal building.

The customs official whisked me through without checking my baggage. 'What is the purpose of the visit, memsahib?'

When I explained that I had come to study their religion and to visit a holy man in Bangalore, his black eyes sparkled as he grinned, baring red and brown teeth stained from chewing betel nut. 'Very good. Very good. Very pleased. Our young ones are turning away from such things and you rich and wealthy Westerners come here to our poor land. It is a remarkable thing. I hope our Mother Bharat looks after you.'

Outside the terminal I was besieged by a group of shouting, khaki-clad taxi drivers. Some began tugging at my backpack, others grabbed hold of my arms and shoulders, reminding me of a group of brown, squawking birds, swooping to grab some spoil. I charged ahead, shaking off their hands, and on reaching the nearest taxi, crawled inside and slammed the door. When I peered back through the window at my assailants, most of them had turned away and were swooping on other arrivals. A few were squatting on the ground, staring at me with curious looks on their faces. I waved at them. They grinned and laughed and began talking amongst themselves. Realising he had a passenger, the driver ran towards the taxi, jumped inside and we drove away. He shouted 'Where to, memsahib?' 'The Ever Happy Guest House', (a hotel I had got from the guidebook Planet Earth) was my reply.

The old taxi that looked to be of 1930 vintage threaded its way through shadowy figures, bicycles, other taxis and rickshaws while the driver pressed his hand down on the horn continuously. There was little street lighting but I could just make out shacks and huts overlapping each other and looking as though they had been built from scavenged scraps. I was intrigued by this and remembered a phrase from somewhere describing the dwellings of India's poor as 'monuments to ingenuity'.

When we finally pulled up at an old building on the edge of the city, the driver turned around and beamed. 'Five hundred rupees, memsahib.' This was about fifty dollars for a ride that should have been no more than two dollars. I shook my head and offered him twenty rupees. The driver grinned. '*Baksheesh, baksheesh*, memsahib?' I handed him another two rupees and clambered out dragging my orange backpack after me. The driver gave me what looked like a salute, spun his taxi around and sped off. I glanced at my watch and noticed it was 12.30 a.m. My first morning in India.

A *charpoi* (rope-strung bed), stretched out onto the pavement, blocked the entrance to the hotel. Someone covered by a thin white sheet was lying on it and snoring loudly. I shook the mound several times and after a few grunts a man's head appeared, eyes squinting. He snorted, leaned over the side of the *charpoi* and spat on the ground, just missing my feet. I managed a smile and asked him for a room. He sat up slowly, shuffled to the door and unlocked it with one of the many keys that dangled from a long string wrapped around his waist. I crawled over the *charpoi* tugging my backpack after me. The man then turned suddenly and barked, 'Husband, kahan hai?' When I explained I didn't have one, he flung his arms in the air and groaned, rolling his eyes upwards.

My room was small with no windows and no furniture except for a *charpoi* in one corner. There was no bathroom and I was told that the communal toilet and shower were at the end of the hallway. An old and dirty ceiling fan draped with cobwebs creaked overhead, a few cockroaches darted across the floor. I sat on the edge of the *charpoi* and unpacked my sleeping bag. It occurred to me that a few months ago I would have been appalled by such surroundings but these days nothing seemed to bother me. Since changing directions in my life I was not only happier but remarkably detached as well. I fell asleep that early morning lulled by waves of excitement. Soon I would see Sai Baba.

Later that day I caught a plane to Bangalore. Even though this was my first journey away from New Zealand, I was not very interested in looking at the scenes and sights of this new country. I felt instead as if I was in some way watching a movie and the scenes on the screen were having little impact on me. Something like the madness of being in love had made me practically oblivious to the world around me.

On arrival I wasn't at all surprised to learn that Sai Baba was at his Brindavan Ashram not far from Bangalore, even though he spent some time on tour in other parts of India or at his other residence, Prasanthi Nilyam, in Puttaparthi. Of course he would be there. He knew I was coming. He would be waiting for me. My excitement at soon seeing him was becoming so strong I was beginning to feel dizzy.

The Brindavan Ashram was situated at a place called Whitefield about sixteen kilometres from the city of Bangalore. I arrived there by scooter rickshaw only minutes before Sai Baba's evening *darshan*. Inside a large compound bordered by a high stone wall, thousands of people were sitting cross-legged on the bare ground, men separated from women.

Most of them were sitting there silently, hardly moving, their eyes glued to the entrance to Sai Baba's residence.

I tiptoed over to the end of one of the many rows and sat down on the hard dusty ground. Devotees acting as guards were standing at the end of each row but most of the time they were also watching the gate. There was an eerie silence and a calm as if we were all suspended in timeless space, a place that didn't belong to this earth world. My heart began to thump erratically.

Glancing up I noticed the sun resting on the mountains in the distance, tinging the sky with orange and pink and just a few seconds later I caught sight of another flash of orange. An orange-robed figure was moving slowly and gracefully out of the gate and a hushed sigh swept through the crowd. It was Sai Baba. He began to walk towards us. I found that my eyes were transfixed on his feet as they glided over the earth, scarcely seeming to touch the surface and it amazed me that he didn't trip over the end of the long robe that lapped over his feet and trailed behind him.

When I looked up at his face I was sure I detected a soft glow and there seemed to be a luminous aura circling his mound of black kinky hair. As I had never seen such a phenomenon before, I wondered whether some psychic facility had recently developed within me. His head was large in proportion to the rest of his body, which was slim and almost dainty. Multiple chins hung above his very short and thick neck. There was nothing extraordinary about his physical features — in fact they could be considered by some as rugged and coarse. But he was God in human form; of that I had no doubt.

When he reached the end of the crowd, he paused to speak to several of the devotees. He slowly moved across the group, occasionally pausing to receive letters. Often he waved his right hand around in circles and distributed what I presumed was the magical ash or *vibhuti* that Stanley Roberts had described to me back in Auckland. Remarkable healing properties have been attributed to this ash as devotees have claimed it cures a wide variety of ailments. People either eat it (with reverence) or rub it on an injured or sick part of the body. By the time Sai Baba was a few feet away from me I could see him clearly producing this ash as if from thin air. His sleeve was pushed right up his arm and with a few circular movements of his forearm, a pile of white-grey ash would appear in his outstretched palm. I watched incredulously and then looked up at his face as I waited for him to acknowledge me, welcome me home.

But he walked past with out so much as a glance in my direction. My heart sank. I was stunned. As I watched him moving away my disappointment faded with the thought that I'd be blessed in days to come. Perhaps he was just testing my faith. Within minutes Sai Baba had disappeared back through the gates. I noticed the sun had finally sunk behind the distant mountains leaving a trail of orange and pink hues. Some of the women near me were weeping and sighing, others remained sitting silently with blissful smiles on their faces. A few began to sing a *bhajan* (a song of praise). What a remarkable place, I thought as I sat there staring at the last spot where I had seen that orange robe before it disappeared from view.

I found a place to stay in a small village about ten

minutes walk away from the ashram. The one room that was available was one of four in a building that had recently been built on the edge of the village. There were three other such buildings in this village and also four more in another village nearby. These had all been built to accommodate the influx of Western visitors, most of whom could not afford the higher costs of hotels or guesthouses in the city of Bangalore itself. The rooms were small — about eight feet square — with low ceilings. Empty, they looked like concrete boxes with only a small grilled window and wooden shutters rather than panes of glass. This lodging cost me only 50 rupees (five dollars) a month, which seemed to me a pittance but not for an Indian whose average weekly wage was evidently about 25 rupees.

My room overlooked a wide expanse of brown and green fields that at first I thought was going to be very restful. Then I discovered they were used as an open toilet area for the whole village including the Western visitors. I was appalled to discover this but reminded myself that there was now no room in my life for negativity. Whatever I had once regarded as distasteful I now had to tolerate or detach from. During the past few weeks my mind had mostly been saturated with love and joy and on the few occasions negative thoughts had entered, I had found it easy to get rid of them.

Within days I had made my concrete dwelling cosy and comfortable. Several trips were made into Bangalore to purchase matting, a mosquito net, a straw broom, buckets, a kerosene stove and other items needed for cooking as well as Indian clothing — petticoats, *choli* blouses and several colourful soft saris. Many people said I looked like an Indian woman in these clothes as I have an olive complexion and dark brown eyes. I began to wear my long black hair tied back as Indian women do. I felt completely at ease in these clothes. They were not only comfortable but wearing them I felt feminine. This was a real change for me because at uni I had worn mostly daggy jeans and T-shirts, sometimes with old overcoats hanging down to the ground. Before that, in my early teens I made sure I was dressed in the latest fashion to attract boys' attention. In contrast, this new Indian way of dressing that made me more attractive and feminine was not for the purpose of attracting men. That hunting game was over for me now. I had read that Indian women dress to be beautiful for their own sake as well as to please their husbands and that in an ideal traditional marriage the husband worships the wife as a goddess rather than as a sex object or piece of property.

Most of the Westerners who lived out in this village had been with Sai Baba for months, a few even for years. The majority were young women in their twenties. But at the daily *darshans* there were about three hundred Westerners most of whom stayed in Bangalore in more comfortable accommodation. They were mainly from America, Japan, or Australia and had come in groups for short visits of one to three weeks. I was surprised to see many older people in these groups and some looked to be in their seventies or eighties. Perhaps my parents would even come here one day.

I became friendly with only a few girls living out in the villages, including a girl, Dawn, who lived in an adjoining room. Many of the Westerners did not seem to go out of their way to make social contact with each other since their whole purpose seemed to be seeing Sai Baba at *darshan* and becoming absorbed in his image for the rest of the day. Some people even adopted the spiritual discipline of *mouna*, maintaining silence. This meant that they could not speak to anybody at all sometimes for days, even weeks.

Dawn was from Australia and had been here five months. She had very pale skin mottled with large freckles and wore glasses. Her thin, straight hair was pulled tightly away from her thin face and tied in a ponytail. She often scowled or frowned but when she spoke about Sai Baba, a softness crept over her face and her small, hazel eyes lit up behind her rimmed glasses. She was shy and did not talk very much but I felt relaxed with her.

For three months my life slowed down and I learned the way of being a *bhakta*, a devotee. In this world, in this little village where time has stood still for centuries, I forgot about the outside world ruled by clocks and timetables and influenced by television and newspapers. Each day revolved around attending *darshan* for it was considered that to be in the presence of the *avatar* was the most important thing for spiritual development. Hence there were no hatha yoga or meditation classes, no regular studying of scriptures and no disciplines to follow except those that an individual chose to adopt on a personal level. Some general guidance was given in the books written by Sai Baba where there was often mentioned the need to be 'pure and virtuous'. He himself wore the traditional orange robe of the Hindu celibate renunciate.

Every day I walked with Dawn through the heavy summer heat along the long dirt path lined with tall trees, crowned with brilliant orange and red flowers, to Brindavan Ashram, the abode of the *avatar*, the incarnation of God. We would spend hours sitting on the hard parched ground in the compound waiting, waiting for Sai Baba to appear — an orange sun gliding from behind the tall, white wall. There were no stipulated times for his *darshans*. He appeared and disappeared twice a day at varying times.

During *darshans* he would single out a select few and wave them towards his residence where private interviews were held. Usually those selected were Indians and most of the Westerners granted interviews were those who had come with a group tour organised by a Sai Baba branch back in their home countries. However each day I sat hoping that on that day Sai Baba would look directly at me and with a flourish of his hand wave me towards his dwelling. But each day he walked past and ignored me. Some of the devotees who received no invitation to a private interview considered this to be a blessing as they rationalised that Baba was working on us at a higher level. I wanted to believe this. I also hoped that one day my time would come or perhaps I would become so pure and strong that his apparent rejections would cease to bother me.

A few devotees sat at Brindavan for most of the day. They sat there waiting and most of the time simply watched the gate of Sai Baba's residence. Sometimes they would sigh rapturously, or their eyes would roll backwards so only the whites showed. Dawn once explained: 'They're in a deep state of *samadhi*. Super consciousness. Like a cosmic orgasm. It often happens to me at night-time and I spend the whole night sitting up, without sleeping. It's really incredible. You wait. When it happens to you, you'll never ever want to leave here. Nothing matters any more.' I thought how wonderful it sounded and hoped that soon such an experience would be mine.

Daily I watched the manifestation of *vibhuti* and sometimes I witnessed sweets, necklaces and rings miraculously appear in the palm of Sai Baba's hand. On one festive occasion, he produced a small statue of Lord Krishna. I never saw any sick or crippled person healed, but I heard countless stories of such miracles occurring. Some devotees claimed that *vibhuti* actually fell out of the pictures they had of Sai Baba on their private *puja* places but I never witnessed this. Yet I still believed these stories. It was strange that I believed all these things so easily, especially as the subject at university that I had excelled in was Research Methodology, where we explored and analysed scientific processes. But I had reached the conclusion that science is limited and unable to measure or prove the existence of spiritual phenomena.

Outside the gates of Brindavan there were always crowds of beggars, some of whom were grotesquely deformed. To assist them in their begging (their only form of income), parents evidently amputate one or more of the limbs of their children at birth or sometimes kept their limbs twisted and bound into travesties of the human form. Mutilated amputees evidently earn more money than fellow beggars who still have limbs intact. The general consensus was to ignore these beggars. Dawn assured me that it was merely their *karma*. Guards were always posted at the outer gates to prevent any of them entering and we were encouraged not to give them any food or money. At first I thought this was cruel and inhumane but, soon, like the others, learned to ignore these sights. I didn't want doubts to disturb my faith.

Apart from sitting and waiting, our time was spent in the purchasing and preparation of food (vegetarian of course) and included fruit, *chapattis*, vegetables, milk, rice, and lentils. Washing clothes was by hand and all water used in cooking and washing was collected by bucket from the central village well. I bathed by squatting down on the floor in the corner of my room with a bucket and a plastic jug. The water would run out through a small hole about three inches square that led outside into a roughly dug open drain that I had to step over whenever I walked out the door.

At least once a week Dawn and I would go into Bangalore to buy provisions or visit our favourite haunt, a milk bar called Jo-Jo's that was run by an American lady who had married an Indian. Here we would pass time sitting on bar-stools, chatting and eating milk sweets or toasted sandwiches, and drinking Indian tea (*chai*) or *lassis* — cold drinks whisked from yoghurt, water, sugar and flavouring of some kind. The American owner was called Joanna and I often wondered why she was never at *darshan* out at Brindavan. I presumed she was a devotee of Sai Baba but concluded that she must be too busy running this shop. She seldom became involved in conversation with us but was friendly and as we were regular visitors she soon came to know our names.

Even though Dawn was a person of few words, some of the other devotees talked or raved a lot. There were always stories to be heard about miracles and healings, including some they had experienced themselves. I listened to most with astonishment and sometimes envy. But I soon discovered most of the devotees seemed to think Sai Baba was somehow involved or had a part to play in virtually everything that happened to them. There were no coincidences, only miracles. No misfortunes or disappointments, only divine testings. If they were late and missed *darshan* this would be construed as Baba testing them and if they were lucky enough to be at Brindavan at the time Baba made an appearance, this was seen as divine grace. Even though I believed Sai Baba was God-incarnate it was still difficult for me to imagine he was actually at the centre of everything and the cause of all things that happened to me. Not only this, the words that were a part of the language of the devotees sometimes irritated me — words such as grace, cleansing, subtle, and purification. Even Dawn used them. When I tried to use such words they never sounded right. Perhaps the others were more spiritually advanced and soon I would be more like them and able to use these words with ease.

Back at the village or at Brindavan I sometimes found myself crying for long periods for no apparent reason. I noticed that many of the other young Western girls wept openly, especially at *darshan*. Occasionally some of the men and some of the older people, including Indians, cried. Sai Baba seemed to have that effect on people. But most of the time I felt happy and considered myself fortunate to be here, saved from the perils of worldly life. Whenever doubts arose, I would push them down again as mere manifestations of my lower mind, best ignored.

However, there were a few occasions when I watched Sai Baba gliding out from his mansion and I wondered what on earth I was doing here sitting like a beggar endlessly waiting for some alms from heaven. I would look at Sai Baba's face and sense some darkness there, an almost demonic expression. But minutes later I would be taken over by euphoric anticipation and then I would think that I must have just been projecting some dark force hiding in the depths of my mind waiting to disturb my peace, my faith. I often wondered why Dawn never expressed any doubts and never seemed to be negative, at least where Sai Baba was concerned.

Each day I hoped that at the next *darshan* Sai Baba would acknowledge me. But he didn't. For three months he neither looked at me nor spoke to me, let alone granted me an interview. Only on one occasion did he walk right up to me until his robes brushed against my feet. Then his feet slid from underneath his robe and his toes began to stroke and caress my feet. I was overcome with emotion, and tears of joy began to roll down my face. Afterwards when I told Dawn what had happened, she looked at me nonchalantly, 'Oh, he used to do that to me all the time. But now he only works on me on deeper, inner levels'.

For three months I could not imagine being anywhere else and expected to live here indefinitely.

But during the fourth month I began to feel restless. Why wasn't I changing? I had expected that after coming here a remarkable transformation would take place in me and that I would be completely taken over by cosmic forces. Even though there had been a drastic change in my life in January, I was waiting for yet another spiral upwards. Was *darshan* and being in the presence of a master all that was necessary for spiritual development? We were given no practices to follow, no work to do, no meditation techniques or special *mantras*. I began to wonder what it would be like to actually live in a traditional Hindu ashram, with strict discipline and routines to follow and more isolated from the outside world.

Not long after the emergence of this restlessness, I fell ill. I woke up one night with my head hot and throbbing and with cramping pains building up in my stomach. I was sweating heavily; my bedclothes and the sari petticoat I used as a nightdress were saturated. Somehow I dragged myself up, grabbed a torch and just made it to the nearby paddocks. At the sight of blood and mucous, I groaned. These were the signs of dysentery.

For three days I lay on my straw mat on the bare concrete floor, sometimes lapsing into a semi-conscious state. Constantly I had to drag myself out on all fours to relieve myself. Occasionally Dawn or another devotee would come in and wash my face with a wet flannel or mix me some Glucolyte to drink. Dawn tried to reassure me. 'Baba's really working on you now. It's his divine grace. He's just cleaning out your body. It happened to me when I first arrived here.' I cringed and restrained myself from snapping or snarling at her. She always spoke softly and her soft voice, quite apart from the words she spoke, was beginning to irritate me. At times I wished that I could jump up and shake her to get some life, some anger, into her.

Most of the time I was left to lie there alone, and for the first time in many months a dark cloud of negativity began to cover me, slowly creeping over my mind. I felt wretched and miserable as I lay on that hard floor and longed to be back at my parents' house with clean white sheets, a soft mattress, a proper pedestal toilet, a bath, running water and my mother caring for me. Often I slept and drifted into strange, murky dreams. There were three in particular that were so vivid that afterwards, for some time, I wondered whether in fact I had been awake and that they were hallucinations or visions.

In the first, I was floating and dancing in the sky with Sai Baba. I was in a blissful state as, naked, we embraced and moved together through soft white clouds. I was feeling intense sexual arousal and had a deep almost unbearable longing for an orgasm but just when I thought he would enter me he would disappear, dematerialise. This happened time and time again. It was as if Sai Baba had assumed the role of Krishna, the Hindu god who teases and woos the *gopis* in a *lila* of divine love. At times when I looked into his eyes, it was like looking through into the universe, into galaxies of stars sparkling and planets revolving. His skin felt like velvet, his body moved freely and gracefully like a young child's. I felt complete ecstasy, my heart seemed to be exploding with love.

When I awoke from this dream my mouth was open in a deep sigh and my face felt soft and light.

For hours afterwards I lay there feeling as if I was bathing in the sweet aftermath of an explosive orgasm.

This intensely pleasurable dream was followed by two disturbing, mysterious ones. The setting for one was a tall, multi-storied hospital. It was old and dirty. I remember going up and down cage-like lifts that clanged and groaned on their cables and pulleys. Then I was lying in a hospital bed, having just given birth to a baby. A nurse strode in, grabbed the baby from out of my arms and took it behind a glass window in front of me. Behind the window there was a crowd of people I had known at some time in my life. Some were relatives of mine; others were former teachers and university lecturers. They were all standing still, expressionless, staring at me. Then some scowling doctors and nurses, holding large knives, walked across to the nurse and, as if in a wild frenzy, began to plunge these knives deep into the baby after which they proceeded to cut off its limbs. I lay on the bed, horrified and unable to move. I tried to scream but no sound came. The crowd of people was still standing there but now they were all grinning at me.

After waking from this dreadful dream, the images persisted in my mind and brought fresh horror and anguish. Soon afterwards I sank into another dream that brought no relief.

In this third dream, I was sitting in the front row waiting for Sai Baba. As I sat there, images of a gigantic long penis, resembling the head and neck of an ancient dinosaur, kept crossing my mind. When Sai Baba came through the gate he was floating about six inches off the ground. The monstrous penis I had been imagining was actually bursting through a large hole in his robes. Approaching the crowd and circulating amongst the devotees, this penis-monster nudged and caressed people. I sat there frozen in terror. In the dream, I believed Baba would know about these fantasies and I was scared of what he might do to me. Perhaps he would cast me out and forbid me to return to the ashram. I closed my eyes and tried to push these dreadful images out of my mind. I wondered whether perhaps Sai Baba was curing me of some demon or monster in my subconscious. But when I opened my eyes, Baba was still floating and his organ was still mingling with the crowd.

I awoke from this dream sweating profusely. I felt confused and bewildered but tried to reassure myself that this sickness, this dysentery and these last two dreams were Sai Baba's grace. He must be curing me at some very deep levels and perhaps I should feel grateful.

The following day I began to feel better. I made fewer journeys to the neighbouring field and was able to sit up for short periods to read or write. I felt excited at the prospect of returning to Brindavan and seeing Sai Baba again. Surely now, after the terrifying descents into hell of my lower mind, he would finally acknowledge me.

But at my first *darshan* after this illness he walked past me and ignored me. I felt devastated. How long could this go on and why was he just working on me at a subtle level, I brooded? I so much wanted him to smile at me and talk with me. As I sat there wallowing in self-pity and rejection, I decided to go into Bangalore alone, without Dawn, for a chocolate milkshake. Perhaps going into the city would distract me. I felt frightened that those morbid states of mind, which had so often darkened my previous life back in Auckland, could creep back again. Surely I had transcended those lower states of pettiness and depression.

As I walked into Jo-Jo's, I stumbled over the end of my sari. Flushed, I looked up to see Joanna grinning at me, 'Oh hi, Mary. How are you going? Still one of them?' I was puzzled and asked her what she meant. 'Oh well, I thought you'd have left by now. You never looked as though you quite belonged to that cult. You never raved on like most of them. They're all loopy, if you ask me.'

The words loopy and cult stung me. I felt slightly insulted. Surely I had been a sincere and serious devotee except for the dreams and doubts that had surfaced during my sickness. But I had been vulnerable then. Surely she didn't think Baba himself was a fraud? It had never occurred to me that anyone who had the good fortune to go near Baba and have his holy *darshan* would not believe that he was a godman, an *avatar*. When I questioned her further, she flung back her head and laughed raucously. 'Are you off your head? He's just a magician. Look, you idiot, there are plenty of people like him all over India. He's just developed occult powers. That's all. Look, I've been here five years now, running this place. I've seen thousands of Westerners come and go. And I've seen the weirdest things happen to them. Some have completely cracked up and ended in mental hospital. And there's been the odd suicide.'

'But look at all the miracles he does'. I noticed my voice had changed. It was like a tiny squeak.

'Mary. Wake up! He's just a hypnotist. Can't you see? He cons rich Americans for their money. Where do you think he got the money from for all the colleges he builds everywhere? Not only that, he's a homosexual. And a hermaphrodite.'

I froze. The few Indians sitting next to me along the counter had all turned towards us, listening intently. Joanna made no effort to lower her voice. I asked her what she meant by a hermaphrodite having never heard the word before, though it sounded as if it was some type of insect. I felt foolish.

'Are you kidding? Where in the hell did you go to school? He's got a vagina as well, you nong! What do you think he plays at with all the young boy students in his fancy colleges? And his rich American devotees. And he probably would like to be with some Western women but I bet he's frightened he might get one of them pregnant. Much safer with men.' She burst into laughter.

My brain felt as if an electric shock had passed through it, fusing the circuits. But at the same time I felt as if I had been jolted awake. It was as if one part of my brain had closed down and another part had been reactivated. I suddenly felt as if I was a different person.

I believed her. As simply as that. In just a few seconds my faith completely vanished. I began to feel devastated. The man I had been worshipping as God incarnate was in fact a sexual pervert. I remembered the dream I had had about Sai Baba's penis whilst I was sick and realised it must have been a warning. I must be getting psychic, I thought. That, at least, was some consolation.

But then panic set in. I thought of the village and all my possessions there. I had to get back, retrieve my belongings and escape. I was trembling as I got up from the stool. I thanked Joanna and muttered something about getting away, getting out of it all. Tears began to sting my eyes. There was a choking sensation in my throat. I wanted to howl.

'Good luck. Don't get sucked back in,' Joanna said. She had stopped laughing now. She looked a little concerned that she had told me the truth, bizarre as it was. As I looked at her I took in her freckled cheeks, her wild red hair curling in all directions, and I thought she was the sanest person I had set eyes on for the past few months. It was as if I had finally woken up. She looked alive, more real than all those besotted Baba devotees that I had been hanging around with. But what about the experience I had at the Henderson Yoga Ashram, the one I thought had changed my life for good? Was that a delusion too? Was all that happiness and joy that had entered into my life just a mirage? What had happened to me and what would happen to me now? Would I go back to being the miserable, lonely and depressed Mary Garden I used to be? That would be unbearable. Everything seemed to be crumbling and crashing down around me. Godless. I grabbed my bag and rushed out of the shop and hired a scooter rickshaw to take me back to the village.

My heart was beating wildly and a choking sensation in my throat was growing as we careered over the dusty, rocky road towards Whitefield. The ride seemed bumpier than usual and I kept on being thrown up from my seat to hit my head on the metal bar overhead. I kept glancing at my watch nervously. The hands didn't seem to be moving. Would we ever get there, I thought frantically. A dull, thudding sensation was beginning to traverse my head and thoughts clashed as they raced through my mind.

When we reached the village I leapt out and yelled to the driver to wait. As soon as I got to my gloomy room, I grabbed my orange backpack, threw most of my possessions inside and put all the trinkets and pictures I had been collecting into a string bag. Whereas my backpack had been half-empty when I left New Zealand it was now full. How could I have stayed in such a dismal and primitive environment, I thought as I glanced around me. I must have been out of my mind. I stumbled outside leaving all my cooking gear, buckets, mats and food where they were. I would have liked to give them to some of the native villagers but there was no time for that.

I noticed Dawn and another girl walking across the faeces-splattered field. 'Hey, Mary, where are you going? What on earth are you doing?' Without looking back, I bolted to the rickshaw and shouted that I was going back to reality, back to the real world. I had woken up at last. I gave a vacant laugh that must have sounded slightly maniacal. Leaping into the rickshaw, I shook the driver by his shoulder. 'Chalo, chalo, Bangalore, Ji.' We sped off in a cloud of dust. When we got about a hundred yards away, I glanced behind me, but they were nowhere in sight. I had expected Dawn to chase after me to try and change my mind and restore my faith. Breathing deeply, I sank back into the seat.

We passed Brindavan. I looked at the clusters of beggars with their mutilated limbs and stumps and the tin cans that were hung over them. I wished I had given them more. Sai Baba could have helped them, I thought, with all the donations and gifts he got from wealthy devotees. Towering behind the wall, I caught sight of his whitewashed dwelling, luxurious by Indian standards, and the tall trees with their red, flame flowers mantling the green. I thought that it was a disgrace that he could live in such a place, while beggars in dirty, torn rags waited nearby for a few coins to purchase food. Above the beggars, monkeys sat on the wall or swung out from the trees as they waited for offerings of food. I remembered seeing Indians throw bananas to these animals and yet walk past the beggars, ignoring them. Perhaps those Indians were devotees of Hanuman, the Hindu monkey-god. I also remembered the occasions when Sai Baba's personal elephant was paraded, showered with flowers, and given delicacies to eat as if she was Ganesh, the elephant-god of learning and propitiousness.

As we crossed the small bridge, on the other side of the ashram, I dragged out the string bag and threw out the glossy pictures of Sai Baba and the trinkets. The pictures caught in a breeze and sailed up into the air and down to a nearby field. I caught glimpses of Baba in flight. He looked evil now. What could have possessed me to think he was God-incarnate? There had to be something wrong with me, some madness, to have been caught up in such a cult in the first place.

Then I caught sight of a group of half-naked children running towards the objects I had chucked out. The children were laughing and yelling in delight. I managed a slight laugh, thinking they would probably sell them to another gullible Westerner.

Chapter 3

Changing Tracks

Even though no one followed me into Bangalore, I had the feeling I was being chased. Perhaps it was the fear that the personality change that had taken place some months ago, and had led me to the Devil himself would happen once again. And once more I would lose sight of reality. As well as this, I sensed other fears emerging that I was too frightened to look at, let alone understand. I pushed them under and donned a mask of courage as I tried to pick up the pieces of my life.

For two days I stayed at the Nataraj Hotel. This hotel was in an area of Bangalore where I thought few, if any, Sai Baba devotees would be staying. During this time I made preparations to travel by train to Madras and up to Delhi. From Delhi I planned to go overland to Europe, but I had no idea what I wanted to do there. I just wanted to escape from India and get as far away from Sai Baba as possible. I decided that going back to New Zealand was out of the question. I didn't want anyone from my past to see me in such a wretched state.

One of the first things I had done on arriving in India was to change most of my travellers cheques into rupees because at that time, in my dreamy state of mind, I had expected to stay in India for the rest of my life. Now I would have to change most of my money back into American dollars because travellers are not allowed to take Indian currency out of the country. Because I had not kept the original exchange receipts that the banks issue, I could not do this legally. It had to be done on the black market.

I made many visits to a local tailor to have some Western-style clothes made up. The remainder of my time was spent roaming the bazaars looking for sweetmeats and other delicacies to eat or sitting in *chai* shops drinking copious cups of *chai*. I tried not to think about recent events and tried to ignore the depression that seemed always to be in the background, like a dark, dense cloud hovering nearby.

During these two days in the city, I felt like a mouse scurrying about. At the first sight of anyone who looked as if they might be a Western devotee of Sai Baba, I would dart into the nearest shop and busy myself pretending to look at the merchandise. I was paranoid at the prospect of such a meeting for I was convinced that if I met up with any of these devotees, they would treat me as a traitor or perhaps they would pretend to be friendly to me and try to lure me back into their cult.

On my last morning in this city, I went for several walks down the narrow alleys near my hotel, laden with all my Indian clothing and trappings. I handed these out to beggars but was surprised at their apparent lack of gratitude. They either asked me for more or asked for money instead. But I also knew that I was just using them as rubbish bins for things no longer wanted.

Now no longer under the spell of Sai Baba, I had begun to notice the poor and destitute of India, their frantic wailing and pestering, the miserable hovels some of them lived in — lean-tos made of cardboard, sacking or scavenged tin. Many just slept in their rags on the footpaths and in the gutters. All the children had runny noses, many looked as if they had eye infections and some of the younger ones left trails of diarrhoea in their paths. Babies and toddlers were often carried around on the hips of siblings who themselves looked as young as five or six years. Even though Bangalore is considered one of the more affluent and pleasant cities of India, and is often referred to as the Garden City, there still seemed to be hordes of beggars that followed and chased me everywhere.

That afternoon I packed my things and went to the station two hours early to make sure I got a seat. But many other people had the same idea. The platform was crowded with bustling travellers and their porters as well as many who looked as though they were camping there permanently. Some were cooking food on kerosene stoves and the smells of strong, pungent spices such as coriander, chilli and cumin drifted through the air. Other people were stretched out on unrolled bedding and were either asleep or just lolling there and talking to those around them. I squatted near the edge of the platform and tried to ignore the mayhem around me: the shouting and hustling, beggars crawling or dragging themselves along the ground and the odd person singing or playing a musical instrument.

The train arrived half an hour after it was supposed to depart. Even before I first caught a glimpse of the train coming, a crowd engulfed me. I pushed and struggled through the entangling mass.

When the train finally reached the platform, I pushed my way through to the nearest carriage, grabbing the only window seat vacant. Within no time, the compartment was overflowing. It was designed to seat twelve people, but there were over fifty crammed inside by the time the train laboured out of the station. One man had even curled up on the floor. One boy, who looked to be no more than eight or nine, was alone and perched on the window ledge holding onto the bars of the window with one hand. Apart from the number of people aboard, there were also mounds of luggage, most of it bedding — mattresses, sheets and pillows — all enclosed in bulky canvas covers. Some of the passengers had even brought along kerosene stoves, pots and pans. Virtually every traveller had at least one carrier of *tiffin* carriers full of foodstuffs.

Within minutes, the train had left the outskirts of Bangalore and was heading eastwards. Smoke began to fill the air from the *beedi* cigarettes and the noise steadily increased: people laughed, talked loudly even sometimes shouted. Some sang songs and occasionally one of the men would play a tune on a flute. Sometimes they would glance at me, laugh or make comments I couldn't understand. I sat there, pressed my face against the bars of the window and tried to block out the noises around me as well as the confusion that was in my head. During the last two days whenever I had thoughts of Sai Baba and his Brindavan Ashram and the absurd way I had behaved, I would feel overcome by apprehension and remorse. I would quickly push away such thoughts for fear I might break down completely.

Night fell a few hours after the train's departure and most of the inhabitants of the compartment began to drift off to sleep. Some, however, continued to talk amongst themselves and this noise was joined with snorting and snoring. Every so often, I squirmed on the wooden slatted seat and tried, often in vain, to change my position. I would drag pieces of clothing out of my backpack and squeeze them under my aching buttocks. All through the night I sat there, sometimes nodding off to sleep for a few seconds, but never for long. There were constant disturbances, particularly from the toilet. The door swung open and shut at regular intervals and dreadful smells wafted out.

I couldn't understand why many of the passengers appeared to be sleeping soundly and in no apparent discomfort. Now I felt ill at ease with Indians, yet strangely enough I had felt close to them when I had first arrived at the Madras airport and during the months I'd spent at Whitefield. My love for India had vanished. I no longer felt fascinated or drawn to her by her religious mysteries or holy men. Now I regarded the Hindu religion with disdain. All that bowing and praying to gods, all that chanting and mumbling. The gods were everywhere in India. One just could not escape them. Their pictures seemed to be in every shop, vehicle and dwelling. They are usually adorned with flowers and incense lit around them several times a day. All these rituals of worship now seemed mindless, pointless and almost absurd. Religion hypnotises, I thought. I didn't want any religion in my life now, even though I felt utterly miserable and lost without it.

The long night passed and morning came. The daylight brought some relief because I could look at the view outside, even though we were only passing through miles and miles of featureless plains. I felt overcome with exhaustion and my head was throbbing. The thought that when I arrived in Madras there stretched before me another thirty hours of third class rail travel to Delhi was almost unbearable. But there was no question of breaking the journey, even for a day in Madras, because I wanted to get out of this country as soon as possible.

Finally the flat stretches of barren landscape gave way to small shacks and huts. I realized we must be approaching Madras. I wrenched my dusty, stained back-pack from under the seat and struggled towards the door, squeezing each footstep between sleeping bodies, baggage and those people who were awake and made no effort to make any room for me to pass. The comment 'Angrezi hippy!' was hissed at me from the corner of the compartment where a few men squatted. They were puffing on thin leaf-encased *beedi* cigarettes. I noticed their black, short hair plastered back with oil and the dark rims of *kajal* on the inside of their eyes, just beneath the eyelashes. They were wearing restrictive Western-styled clothing from the 1950s era — shirts and tight pants. They looked awkward as well as sinister. I sneered at them. Then someone close to me nudged my thigh and whispered creepily, 'Want a kiss, lady?' I pushed myself towards an empty space near the door and threw my backpack down to create a barrier between myself and the other people in the compartment. Tears stung my eyes. I swallowed and breathed deeply. I wanted only to get away from this country and away from these people.

Now that I was no longer dressed in a sari and wearing a kumkum spot on my forehead, young boys and men often shouted stupid things at me. I felt awkward in jeans and T-shirt. People probably thought I was a hippy. Perhaps I should have continued to wear my sari while travelling. I had been told that Western hippies had a bad name in India because of their casual sexual relationships. Uninhibited behaviour between the opposite sexes is especially upsetting to the majority of Indian people as this goes against traditional Hindu culture.

Glancing at my watch, I realized we were three hours late and I would probably miss the Delhi Express. 'Nothing is on time in this country', I thought bitterly. I felt overwhelmed with impatience and restlessness, yet the Indians seemed so patient, a patience that was different from resignation. Perhaps they were just used to waiting. It was a strange country, India. It seemed that everyone was locked into some kind of dream-state, perhaps drugged by the religious rituals that the majority of the people practise at least twice a day.

Dust was billowing through the open windows covering everything with layer upon layer of fine red and brown particles. It made breathing difficult. The dust didn't seem to bother the Indians around me. It was a part of their way of life. They were born into it and lived with it. Nothing seemed to bother these Indian people — not the poverty, the dirt, the noises or the endless waiting. Sweat dripping down my face congealed in the dust to form blobs of mud. I could feel sweat sliding down from my armpits and there was a wet patch at the small of my back. I was so sick of this land of heat and dust.

As the train lurched to a halt, I wrenched the door open and leapt out. I struggled through the crowds and climbed up and down long flights of stairs to various platforms after being misdirected several times by Indians trying to be helpful. But I was horrified when I finally reached the correct platform and saw my train puffing smoke and hooting as it began to edge its way down the track. There seemed to be as many people clinging onto the outside as could have been packed inside. People were even running alongside the moving train to try, mostly in vain, to catch something they could hold on to and hoist themselves on board. Some of the men had clambered onto the roof and were crouching there grinning, with looks of triumph on their faces.

I backed away and struggled to the ticket office. I was told the next train would leave in twelve hours. With my ticket refunded, I searched for a corner of the crowded platform and sat down. Wrapping my arms around my backpack, I rested my head on the top and closed my eyes. I couldn't think clearly. I longed to be able to have a good cry but tears would not come. I had wanted to cry since I broke away from the ashram but somehow it was as if I had cut off these emotions; fear and frustration had overwhelmed me instead.

After what seemed ages, an announcement that there was going to be an extra summer special train, especially for pilgrims on *yatra*, jolted me alert. I was travelling in the *yatra* season, the great migration northwards — a time when thousands of Indians escape the heat and take refuge by the holy rivers or with their gurus in the Himalayas. But even as I reached the ticket office, a surging mass of people was swarming in the same direction. There was no queue, although one harassed railway official tried in vain to organize one. I fought to keep my place in the crowd. Slowly I moved to the front but by the time I reached the window all second and third class tickets had been sold. After purchasing a first-class sleeper for 300 rupees, I walked away thinking that a bit of a luxury would be good. I felt like pampering myself and at last I would be able to lie down and catch up on some sleep.

I walked past a stand displaying books and magazines and wondered whether to purchase something to read on the long journey ahead of me. At a quick glance, most of the material seemed to be either comics or cheap Indian novels about romance or violence. Turning away, I decided to try and sleep most of the way instead.

My carriage was right down at the end of the train and when I clambered aboard I was aghast to find the compartment that was to be my home for the next two days was little more than a cattle truck. A layer of dirt and food covered the walls and the floor. The seats were stained and smothered with dust. There was a very musty smell as if the train had been shut up for a long time. I detected a smell of urine and this made me suspect the train had recently housed beggars with young children or babies. I wiped down the seats with my handkerchief, opened the window and then turned on the small fan perched on a ledge just above the window. This fan only moved on one speed, irrespective of the setting and the blades moved very slowly, creaking at various positions. I sighed and resolved to ignore these physical surroundings as much as possible. At least I would soon be leaving, moving northwards, far away from the influence of Sai Baba.

When the train whistled to signal its imminent departure, I was perplexed as to why no Indian ladies or children had joined me in my compartment because I had only booked one berth and there was one vacant. Realising that since I had been here, no other passengers at all had climbed aboard this particular carriage, I got up and wandered down the aisle inspecting the other compartments. I was astonished to find that they were all completely empty. For a second I wondered whether I had boarded the wrong train. The train lurched forwards and backwards and began to edge its way slowly out of the station. I felt relieved. At least for part of the journey I would be alone. I needed such space and silence after the journey from Bangalore, which had completely assaulted my senses. Maybe, at last, some peace would return to my tired mind.

Madras was soon left far behind and I rested my head back on the seat and listened to the soothing cadence of the train wheels. Up above me on the blotchy ceiling a spider was swinging out from its web. With masterly moves it was fixing the cross-pieces of its intricate trap. Soon some creature, perhaps a fly, would be fighting furiously against the sticky threads being woven around it. At some time it would give up its fight, breathe its last breath, suffocated.

Watching the spider reminded me of Sai Baba and how I had been caught in his trap. I thought about the new personality I had acquired during that time. Now I could hardly connect myself to the way I had behaved and the way I had thought.

Who am I now? Am I the same old Mary Garden or am I someone else? Perhaps this is all a dream or am I just going crazy?

I could not understand why all my peace and joy had vanished. Was it because I had decided that Sai Baba was not a god-man? Perhaps I was being possessed by Baba's demonic powers? Perhaps I had not escaped him at all?

As I sat there, my thoughts began to change direction. I wondered whether perhaps it was Joanna who was the demon. Perhaps she had just heard some idle gossip. Even if she was correct in her allegations, who is to say that holy men can't have sex? What if Baba was an *avatar* after all and in my rejection of him I had also rejected God as well? This possibility seemed plausible and would explain why all my peace and joy had vanished. Or perhaps the devil was in me alone, created by my mad mind. I felt so confused. None of the last few months made any sense. The sooner I was back in the West with its clarity, order and cleanliness the better. Perhaps there I would be able to get a clearer perspective. All these thoughts rushed through my mind, for now there were no outside distractions and disturbances. Now that I was travelling alone, I had only my own miserable mind for company.

I closed my eyes and kept imagining myself running or being pursued. Into my dreamscape Sai Baba appeared, flashing orange, seeking me out. Wide-eyed female devotees, shrouded in long shimmery saris, sprinted past him. They chased me and mouthed entreaties, 'Come back, you're running away from God. Come back we'll save you. Come back or Sai Baba will curse you.' I ran and ran, breathless as they came closer and closer.

Finally I dragged myself up and decided a wash might shake me out of my morbid state of mind. There was no washroom on the train but I managed in the toilet, where water trickled slowly out of a tap. When I had finished, I made my way back to my compartment. In spite of the appalling state the toilet was in, the water had a rejuvenating effect on me and I resolved to make the most of this long journey and concentrate my thoughts on what might lie ahead in this new direction my life had taken.

Every few hours or so the train would lurch to a halt at a station. Sometimes it would stop for no apparent reason and we would wait in the middle of nowhere for up to an hour. Whenever we reached a station there would be a tremendous commotion outside as vendors pushed and fought each other to get to the windows. Many were balancing trays on which were small, irregular-shaped, clay cups of steaming *chai* that looked like dirty dishwater. Others had trays with snacks dotted with occasional small stones and covered with flies.

I stopped thinking about Sai Baba and my life as a devotee but my mind kept sinking into states of lethargy and depression. The day ground past. Time dragged unbearably. I felt as if I had been in this wretched train on the wretched journey forever — in an eternal hell.

As the evening drew near, I watched the fiery sun slip behind the edge of the brown, barren plains. As it began to disappear, darkness covered the bleak landscape and my mind entertained even more fears. Fears that I might be attacked during the night and perhaps have my money stolen. I realized that my body would be the first target of attack either for money or rape or both. Sensible travellers always carry their money close to their body, usually concealed in belts next to their skin or in hidden, inner pockets.

Since I was travelling alone, it seemed wiser to conceal my money elsewhere. After some panicky thought I decided to hide my valuables within the compartment itself. My eyes passed over a paper bag full of raisins and nuts that I had purchased for the journey. 'How ingenious', I thought. 'Who would suspect that my money and passport would be hidden in an old paper bag?' I carefully slid the leather pouch containing all my worldly valuables into the paper bag and then took out my penknife from the outside pocket of my back-pack and tucked it into a concealed pocket on the inside of my blouse. I felt more at ease now.

The world became black outside but inside the compartment there was a dim light from a solitary light bulb that dangled from the ceiling. The light from this would hardly have been bright enough to read from. Suddenly there was a noise outside my compartment. I jumped. But it was only a railway attendant bringing my evening meal, which I had ordered at an earlier station. A tray, or a *thali*, was heaped with soggy white rice around which were placed an aluminium tumbler of water and five small dishes called *catoris*. These *catoris* contained lentils, yoghurt, curried peas, potatoes, carrots and several kinds of chutney. Half a dozen cold *chapattis* were perched on the edge of the *thali*.

Such meals I had already learnt to eat with my right hand, pouring some of the contents of the *catoris* into the bed of rice and then adroitly scooping up morsels of this soggy mixture with my finger tips and throwing these into my mouth before too much fell back onto the *thali* or dribbled down my chin. At times, while eating, my teeth would grind up against a stone or a twig, which I spat out on the floor, the Indian way. The vegetables were highly spiced with red chilli, which I had yet to become accustomed to, let alone enjoy. I waded my way through them because I felt so hungry and because eating might help fill up the dark vacuum inside me. I mopped up the liquid mush remaining on the *thali* with the last of the *chapattis* and stuffed it into my mouth.

With the tumbler of water in my left hand, I poured some water over my right hand to wash it and then gulped down the remaining water to quench the fiery sensation in my stomach. I left the *thali* and tumbler outside in the corridor and locked the door from the inside.

I then made preparations to go to bed. I yanked the back of the seat down and fastened it at each end to the walls to form the upper bunk. I dragged out my sleeping bag (the inside of which was about the only thing not covered by dirt and grime), crawled inside and waited for the comfort of sleep.

After a restless night, I awoke just as the sun was crawling up the sky. Within seconds, I began to sneeze from the dust that danced in the air and was getting up my nose. I reached out to open the shutters of the window. As my hand pulled the latch down, a piercing pain shot through one of my fingers. I screamed loudly. A scorpion was my first thought, but looking down I noticed a gigantic black ant biting and sucking nonchalantly. Then to my horror, looking around, I could see swarms of them trailing across the floor and up onto the bedside table where they were scrambling in and out of the bag of nuts and raisins I had left there the night before. Grabbing the paper bag, I shoved it out of the window.

What a relief! But I was still less than halfway through this gruelling train journey. The thought that in a few days I should be free of this country and all its misery, its confusion and its biting ants was some comfort. I wondered when we would reach the next station so that I could order a Western-style breakfast of eggs, toast and tea. Suddenly I realized what I had just done and began to search frantically through my clothes and possessions hoping against hope that I was mistaken. I began to throw all the contents out of my backpack on the floor and then I scrambled back onto the bunk and groped around my sleeping bag. I buried my head in my hands. I had not only got rid of the ants; I had rid myself of all my money and my passport to freedom!

For a few moments I felt totally disoriented. Then a feeling of helplessness swept over me. My eyes filled with tears and deep sobs racked me. I couldn't stop them. I knew I wasn't just crying for my lost money and passport. I was also crying because I no longer felt spiritual. Since the day I had lost my faith in Joanna's coffee shop, all my joy and happiness had vanished. I had felt the full impact of my physical surroundings during these last few days, yet the noise, the dirt, and the dust had scarcely bothered me when I first arrived in India.

As I cried I also wondered whether I should pull the emergency cord and stop the train. Already precious minutes had passed. How could we ever find the wretched bag now? It could have dropped down anywhere. How absurd I would look if anyone found out that this stupid hippy-westerner had hidden her money in a paper bag and actually thrown it out of the window! The conductor might not even believe me and I might be locked up in some filthy madhouse when the train reached Delhi.

So I just sat there and cried and at times I noticed that my crying was almost a hysterical laugh. Tragic though my predicament was it was also absurd, almost comic. As the sobbing subsided I felt a strange sense of relief sweep over me. The thought came to me that perhaps I was meant to have lost all my money and passport. Perhaps a higher power didn't want me to leave? Perhaps I had a spiritual destiny here after all? As this bizarre conclusion settled in, for the first time in days, I no longer felt alone. I was being looked after. Strangely enough peace and happiness began to fill my mind. Perhaps my loss was not the result of my foolishness but actually divine intervention? As I lay there pondering over this possibility, I drifted off into a deep refreshing sleep.

Some time later I found my face being stroked and caressed by soft silk. Folds and folds of silk brushing gently over me. I sighed, thinking that I was in some kind of heaven. Opening my eyes, I looked upwards and noticed that the swaying, blue folds rose into two enormous breasts and dangling gold necklaces. I shook my head and blinked my eyes. I then realized that a large Indian lady was leaning against the lower bunk arranging her bedding on the bunk above me. As she leant back to the floor to pick something up, I caught sight of her sagging face and sunken eyes, a smudged red kumkum spot on her forehead. She caught sight of me squinting at her. She struggled upright with a few short gasps.

'Ah, you're awake. A foreigner! You're not alone, are you?' I nodded my head. 'Ah, you Westerners are crazy. Destroying our young people. Wandering here and there doing what you like. A very bad influence on our sacred culture with all your loose morals.'

She undid part of her sari and rearranged it more tightly around her bulging middle and swung the end back across those voluminous blue breasts. She sighed loudly and wiped the sweat off her forehead, smudging the kumkum spot even more. The *kajal* lining her eyelids was also smudged and had begun to run down her cheeks. 'Well, talk! Have you lost your tongue? What's your name? Where are you going? What are you doing here in my country?'

I sat up and told her my pathetic story. Everything except the rumours I had heard about Sai Baba and my dream about his penis. She listened intently and often laughed at what seemed quite inappropriate times. She laughed when I told her about running away from Sai Baba. She laughed when I told her that I had thrown my passport and money away. I felt she was laughing at me and began to feel even more sorry for myself. When she laughed it was her whole body that laughed. It shook with gaiety and mirth and all the masses of jewellery on her chest, her fingers, her ear lobes and her nose moved with her.

After a while we were joined by her elderly mother-in-law, who shuffled into the compartment nodding her head up and down continuously as she grinned from a toothless mouth. She wore a plain white sari make from *khadi* cloth. She was assisted by a young man who could have been her son, or perhaps her grandson. When she was seated on the end of my bunk, he placed his hands in prayer position in front of his forehead and bowed to both the younger lady and myself while saying '*Namaste*': the traditional Indian greeting. Kneeling on the ground, he touched the elderly woman's dainty white feet with his hands and then brought his hands up again and bowed to her. He stood up and walked out.

The lady, whose name was Shanti, and her mother-in-law, whom I was instructed to address as Mataji ('Respected Mother'), soon made themselves comfortable next to me with their legs tucked up underneath them. They began chattering away in loud, high-pitched voices throwing their arms and hands around in the air dramatically, shaking their heads and constantly rearranging the end of their saris flung over their shoulders. Shanti did most of the talking and, as they mostly talked in Hindi, I had no idea what they were talking about. They would often laugh loudly and clutch various parts of my body. I presumed that at these times they were talking about me.

In spite of their chatter and laughter, I felt enormously comforted by their presence. Every so often Shanti would struggle down to the floor and squat there as she poured out a drink of water from an earthenware pot into a stainless steel tumbler. This was shared amongst us and we would lift it in turn above our lips with our heads tilted slightly backwards so as to pour the water into our mouths without touching our lips on the rim of the tumbler. Usually, I dribbled some of the water all down my face. They would laugh almost hysterically and I would laugh too. At other times Shanti would rummage amongst layers of stainless steel *tiffin* tins clamped into two upright carriers. These *tiffin* tins contained a wide variety of foods. Most were spicy vegetables, rice and lentils. In some were yoghurt and delicious milk-based sweets.

I soon understood why Shanti was so robust. She ate continuously. She insisted that I share this food with her and on one occasion I felt so full and shook my head when she thrust yet another *catori* of food onto my lap. She became indignant and leant over and pinched my skin through the top of my skirt. 'Look — all skin and bones. Don't you know that we Indians like fat women? It's a sign of beauty in this country. Eat. Eat.' I struggled on but began to eat slowly, for fear I might pass out from overeating or, worse still, vomit all over them.

Towards nightfall, we arranged our bedding so I would sleep on the top bunk and Mataji and Shanti would sleep top and tail on the bottom bunk. Fortunately Mataji was tiny; otherwise they could not have squeezed onto the narrow seat. I kept hoping that Shanti might ask me to stay with them when we reached Delhi. Occasionally I would feel tinges of panic. What would I do when I arrived? I had no money now, nor addresses of places to stay. Once I glanced down at the 18-carat gold watch that my grandmother had given me for my twenty-first birthday. I decided that as a last resort, I could always sell that.

I wondered whether perhaps I should ask Shanti to lend me some money, just enough to take a rickshaw out to the New Zealand High Commission to ask them for help. I had heard stories in Bangalore of Westerners being turned away from their respective embassies. There had been too many drug-addicts creating wild stories to obtain money to sustain their addiction. What if the New Zealand High

Commissioner didn't believe my story and turned me away? Thoughts such as these went round and round in my brain.

How simple my life could be if I could just sit here forever, observing life as it passed by outside, with the constant rhythmic movement of the train and the sound of its wheels clicking underneath. At times I felt like leaping into Shanti's lap and burying myself into those soft mounds of fat and her large melon-like bosoms.

By the following day, as the train approached Delhi, Shanti had not offered me any invitation to stay with them or to lend me some money. I was in a state of panic. Finally in sheer desperation, I plucked up enough courage to ask her if I could borrow a small amount of money. She let out a loud laugh and flung her head backwards. The rolls of fat lapping over her skirt squelched up and down, 'But you might be lying. How do I know your story is true?'

I felt completely stunned. I couldn't believe that she doubted me. I felt angry and wished I hadn't shared all her spicy, rich food. But I smiled sheepishly and offered her my gold watch as a guarantee. I undid the clasp and handed it to her. She grabbed it out of my hand and shuffled up to the window closer to the light. Time and time again she turned it over in her hands. I watched in disbelief. At last she placed it near her chest, closed her eyes and chanted out, 'Om Sri Hanuman, Om Sri Hanuman'. She then pushed the watch down the deep cleavage between her voluminous breasts and drew up the loose end of her sari where there was a lump at one end. She undid the knot and pulled out a bundle of rupees and handed over two fifty-rupee notes. Pulling out a notebook from one of her bags, she instructed me to write down my parents' address. When I had done this she wrote her name and address on another page, tore it out and handed it to me.

Feeling foolish but relieved, I embraced her awkwardly and thanked her over and over again while she patted and thumped me on the back. All through this transaction, I noticed Mataji sitting there silently, her eyes closed whilst she fingered her *mala* beads and muttered some *mantra* over and over.

Once again a tremendous loneliness and despair crept over me. The small taste of peace that I had had the previous day when I imagined a higher power, perhaps God, was looking after me, had long since vanished. Now my life felt like a nightmare. How was I going to escape from this country?

Chapter 4

The Winding Path

After finding a room to stay in a guesthouse in Old Delhi, I spent ten days trying to sort out worldly affairs that had now become very important to me. One of the first things was to make arrangements for a replacement British passport. Fortunately I had decided to leave my New Zealand passport with my mother for safekeeping, so I rang and asked her to send it over. She was relieved when I told her what a wonderful time I was having. My letters home so far had contained glowing reports of my new home, though before leaving Bangalore I wrote to tell her that she was right, after all, about Sai Baba — he was strange and now gave me the creeps.

The New Zealand High Commissioner in Delhi was kind and helpful. As well as agreeing to lend me fifty rupees a day and organizing the replacement of my travellers cheques, he also contacted my insurance company in New Zealand. Evidently they got a good laugh out of my story (and believed me). They agreed to replace the full amount of money I claimed to have chucked out of the window of the train but I instructed them to forward this money to my mother in case I needed it at a later date. The

High Commissioner said to contact him when ever I needed help and that I was welcome to visit him and his wife at their home; perhaps I could have a meal with them if I had time. He was very interested to hear more of my adventures so far.

Everything was starting to work out for me. I felt that I had finally extricated myself from Sai Baba's sticky web. Even though there were times when I felt overwhelmed by the frantic pace of this city, my days were too hectic for me to feel the depression and self-pity that had plagued me during the last days in Bangalore and throughout the two long train journeys. Most of the time I felt an emotional numbness and resigned myself to the fact that life is meaningless after all: there is no God.

I went to make enquiries about cheap journeys overland by bus but was dismayed to learn that fighting had broken out up north and the border had been closed indefinitely. As I didn't have enough money for air travel, there seemed to be no option but to remain in India until the border was reopened. Fortunately I seemed to be forgetting about my bad experiences with Sai Baba and there was no longer the urgency to run away.

But all my plans to leave India and travel to Europe changed one morning. I was strolling along one of the narrow lanes that run off the centre of Paharganj when I came to a Shiva *mandir*, a temple for the worship of Lord Shiva. A ceremony of worship, *arti*, was being held. There were only a few Indian women present and when they saw me standing there they smiled sweetly and *namasted*. I *namasted* to them and we all turned to look at the statue of Shiva. It was a beautiful, gleaming white figure sitting in a lotus position, eyes shut and with a hint of a peaceful smile on its lips. It was life-size and filled the far end of the small, narrow *mandir*.

The *mandir* was spotlessly clean and looked as if it was made out of a grey-white marble. The priest was bending over the statue, streaking its forehead with yellow stripes and then he knelt down and did the same with a small Shiva *lingam* placed nearby. I had been told that many devotees of Shiva worship and pray to this strange phallic-shaped object since it is meant to represent some powerful aspect of God. The one in this temple had red and white flowers scattered around its base. As I looked at it, the priest began to pour a container of *ghee* over its tip. This gluey, thick, white substance, which is considered a luxury by most Indians spilled down the sides and trickled into the flowers.

There was an intense atmosphere in that small *mandir*; the thick, dense air was full of peace and silence. It enveloped me on all sides and seeped into me. As I stood there, a deep relaxation came over me as if I was resting in the aftermath of a powerful orgasm. The priest began to ring a bell and to sing the song of worship (also called *arti*) that is sung in Hindu temples.

Listening to that haunting song invoking the god Shiva, I stood rocking myself backwards and forwards and humming in unison. I closed my eyes and let my full attention drift into the sounds of the priest's voice. The drum beating and the bell ringing merged with it and it seemed as if there was just one sound. My mind emptied of thoughts as I listened. One sound — and no thoughts interfering. I felt enraptured by this glorious sound that seemed so close and familiar to me.

I did not move until the ceremony was over and

then I felt exultant and wanted to jump with joy. I felt deliriously happy and realized that there was God without Sai Baba after all, that there was meaning to my life after all. Faith in something other than myself had been restored. I could not understand what was happening to me but certainly didn't feel like questioning this new state that had welled up in me. I wasn't going to reject happiness when at last it had returned to my meaningless life.

As I walked away, I decided to go to the foothills of the Himalayas to where the Shivananda Ashram was situated. This ashram was the headquarters of the Divine Life organization of which the Henderson Yoga Ashram in Auckland was a branch. I remembered Guruji had mentioned a comfortable and reasonably priced Government Tourist Bungalow (a quarter of a mile away from the ashram itself) where I could stay until given permission to stay at the ashram. He had also told me many stories of how beautiful it was up there with the wondrous sight of the Ganges River weaving its way down through the mountains. I realized also that the mountains would offer some respite from this summer heat. Even though the worst of the heat had passed and the rainy season was approaching, sometimes temperatures still soared up to 39 or 40 degrees Celsius. I then I remembered how Guruji had warned me about Sai Baba, that he was a black magician and the group was a dangerous cult. We had all laughed at him at the time. But he was right after all. Yet after that dinner with Stanley Roberts, where I had become convinced that Sai Baba was God-incarnate, I had even looked down on Guruji and thought he lacked humility. How fickle my mind was!

Within hours of making this decision to go to the Himalayas I had caught a bus to Rishikesh. The bus was so crowded that at times I thought it might roll over. There were people sitting on top of the bus itself, perched on top of the luggage that was loosely tied onto a flimsy-looking luggage rack. Other people hung outside the bus and clung to the rails on the doorway or to the edges of the windows. The roads were dusty and rocky and the bus often had to follow a criss-cross pattern to avoid sleeping buffalo or other animals.

Six hours after we had left Delhi, I caught sight of the Ganges — Ganga as Indians call it. We were approaching Hardwar ('the Gateway to Lord Vishnu'). I leant my head right out of the open window so as I could watch her sparkling, snaking flow rushing steadily downwards. It was enthralling to watch her. My heart leaped whenever we turned a corner and she would come into view: never before had I been so enchanted by a river.

It was still the pilgrim season and the roads were swarming with thousands of Indians who had travelled up there for the sole purpose of bathing and to drink the water from the Ganges. Because at Hardwar the river leaves the mountains and enters the plains, Hindus believe that Ganga's power to wash away sins at this point is supreme. Most of these pilgrims were walking in large family groups and evidently had walked for long distances. There were babies, young children and elderly grandparents. I had been told that for some it is a once in a lifetime pilgrimage.

From Hardwar all the way to Rishikesh some twenty-five kilometres away, I caught glimpses of the Ganges. Before Hardwar she had been relatively smooth and free flowing but now the river was becoming stronger and more beautiful. I felt a deep longing to sit by her, to be near her and to bathe in her waters. The further up we climbed, the clearer her waters became until we neared Rishikesh. Here she was a rich expanse of blue and green bordered by white, sandy beaches. The Himalayas too became greener and richer as they rose up from either side of this great river. These mountains spread far into the distance where they were snow-capped and their outlines blurred and disappeared into the sky. Excitement welled up in me. This was the most beautiful place I had ever seen.

When we reached the village of Rishikesh, I took a horse *tonga* to the outskirts where the Government Tourist Bungalow was perched on a small hill overlooking the Ganges. Along the banks of the river I could see groups of huts with thatched roofs huddled together, with small clusters of swamis in bright saffron or dull ochre robes moving around the huts or sitting near them. There was a slight coolness in the air that seemed to be moving across from the river.

I was given a large room, sparsely furnished with a flat-based wooden bed, a ceiling fan and a small wooden table. The room was spotlessly clean. The first thing I did after signing the register was to wash in the communal bathroom, which was just an empty room with a tap near the floor and a hole in one wall for the water to run out. There was only cold water, but this was invigorating. Afterwards I felt truly clean for the first time in two weeks: days of dusty, dirty train journeys, and ten days of a city blanketed with smoke and dust were washed away.

Walking back to my room, I met the only other

guest at the bungalow. Evidently Indians and many Westerners preferred to stay at the local ashrams or Indian styled hotels in the village of Rishikesh. He was an Australian called Martin, a bulky, friendly man with a shaven head. He wore a pale yellow *lungi* tied roughly around his middle. The upper part of his body was naked. I soon learnt that he had been in India for two years looking for his 'real' guru. He had been to all the well-known god-men and yogis (advanced practitioners of yoga) that Westerners have been flocking to over recent years.

'Most of them are dirty old men though,' he remarked. 'The gurus that is. Some of them even get their female devotees pregnant and take no responsibility. I've heard some dreadful stories about sheilas getting pregnant. Perhaps some of them even die. Who would ever know? Most of them have broken all contact with their families and their parents. Yet whatever happens to them, these devotees still believe in their bloody gurus. They believe it's all their *karma*! You could get them to believe anything. I wouldn't be surprised if some of those gurus have it off with the guys too.'

'I wouldn't be surprised either,' I remarked, thinking of Sai Baba. But I didn't want to think about that bizarre episode in my life; it was still too disturbing. Listening to Martin's tales of the Indian spiritual supermarket, I vowed never to get involved with a guru, let alone have sex with one! I wanted to practise hatha yoga and receive some teachings in this field, but I wanted no one to meddle with my mind or soul again. I wanted to walk on my own path.

'Well, tomorrow I'm going up to the jungle to see this yogi, this Swami Balyogi Premvarni,' Martin continued. 'I've heard some far-out stories about him and he allows only a few people at a time to stay there. He's obviously not into name and fame like the rest of them. This will be my last try. If it doesn't work, I'm heading back to Aussie. You never know, I might be able to learn from the Aborigines. I bet they've got a secret or two that they hide away from the white bastards who took over their land. Maybe they have secrets of the universe that the white fellas are too arrogant to even grasp or explore.'

When I awoke the next morning, Martin had gone. I spent a restful day washing out all of my clothes, sleeping bag and backpack and made one trip into the village to buy a few provisions and toiletries. In the afternoon, I walked down to the Ganges and spent a few hours lying on the white sand listening to the water roar. My mind felt at peace and it seemed as if the nightmare of the last few weeks was truly over. I felt I could stay in this place of beauty and stillness indefinitely.

Martin reappeared towards sunset. I groaned inwardly on seeing him as I could tell from his expression that he had probably found, after all, his 'guru'. For the next two hours he talked about what he called 'this magical garden and this amazing yogi who can look right through you'. He also tried to talk me into going up there the following day during the visiting time between 2 and 5pm. At first I was reluctant but he was so persistent that I finally agreed to go up to the ashram for the walk, on the condition that I wait for him outside at the bottom of the hill that he had described.

The following day just after lunch we set out. We walked up the narrow road towards the Laxman Jhula Bridge. On the way we passed the Shivananda

Ashram — a large, sprawling complex with hundreds of orange-robed, shaven swamis shuffling around. I intended to spend the following day visiting these headquarters and was even going to make enquiries about staying there for a while to practise yoga. Seeing it like this, I changed my mind. It was too crowded and too noisy — not at all the peaceful sanctuary I had imagined. I would stay on at the Tourist Bungalow instead.

The road ended at the Laxman Jhula suspension bridge. The main road up to the higher reaches of the Himalayas branches off just out of Rishikesh and curls upwards through the mountains. It is evidently many miles before the road winds its way down again and follows the route of the Ganges upwards.

Just below the bridge, on the banks of the river, was a leper colony. On the side of the road, just before the bridge, a group of lepers in tattered, stained rags had gathered. Their shrunken stumps were barely covered with shreds and strips of rags; flies covered their disfigured bodies and hovered around them. At the sight of us walking towards them, some of the lepers let out dreadful wailing noises. Others screamed and a few began rolling around on the ground with looks of agony on their faces. I felt completely shaken and stood there for a few moments gaping at them. Clumsily I the reached down under my blouse into the money pouch I had concealed there and took out a few coins, which I threw on the ground in front of them. But at this, some of them went berserk and came leaping or crawling closer to me as they shouted 'ma ma'. They sounded like sheep bleating pitifully. Some of them then threw themselves prostrate down on the ground before me. Aghast, I turned towards the bridge and quickly sprinted away. I didn't stop until I was well onto the swaying, creaking bridge. I waited for Martin, feeling sick and foolish.

When Martin strode up to me, he laughed. 'Look, if you give them your sympathy and money, where will it end? What use will a few coins do? Perpetuate their miserable life by yet another meagre meal? Poverty in India is a bottomless pit. It's best to ignore the beggars otherwise you'll end up like one of them. We're not in a position to help them.'

I glanced back and noticed most of the lepers had disappeared over the hill. A few of those remaining were crouched on the ground and looking at me. They had mischievous grins on their faces.

'Look,' Martin added, 'Most of them are happier than a lot of Westerners. Didn't you see some of their faces? They looked pretty happy to me in spite of the act they were putting on for your sake. They're better off than a lot of our oldies locked away in nursing homes and institutions, drugged up to the eyeballs'.

I hadn't noticed their faces when I was close to them, as I couldn't take my eyes off their diseased stumps. The sight of these sickened me to a much greater extent than the mutilated limbs of the beggars I had encountered previously. The ulcerations on these lepers were exposed and not even adequately bandaged for protection from the hovering flies and whirling dust.

On the other side of the bridge was the small village of Laxman Jhula consisting of a few temples, ashrams and shops catering mostly for tourists and pilgrims. From this village we followed a small dusty track along the river for about a mile and then we took another path that turned inwards and led up into the mountains.

A few hundred yards up this path we came to a large, ornate gate. This was a towering structure about eight feet high. Large spikes protruded from the top of the gate and resting across some of the spikes were two rather gaudy emblems of lotus flowers, painted pastel pink. From the thick, concrete side pillars of the gate ran a barbed wire fence that disappeared into dense trees and bushes. On one of the pillars was a sign that read in Hindi and English, 'International Academy of Yoga'. Beneath this sign hung a wooden notice with the words: 'Visiting times — 2 p.m. to 5p.m.'

There was a concrete bench on the side of the path. I sat down and remarked to Martin that the place looked like a prison. 'Don't be stupid. It's jungle here. They have to keep the wild animals out. Panthers, tigers, wild dogs and monkeys, who knows. They probably don't want sightseers and pilgrims wandering up there at any time disturbing them. This isn't your typical noisy Indian ashram. Just like cheap hotels, most of them. This is a real ashram. A place for retreat and contemplation. Wait until you see one of them. They're advanced beings, I'm telling you. I've never seen anything like it. You can't compare them to the others like those Rajneesh freaks, Muktananda's followers, the Sai Baba loonies and all the rest of them. Look, I've seen them all. They're lemmings. They haven't got minds of their own. The groups they're in are just cults. But this place is unbelievable. A place of real spiritual power.'

I felt irritated by Martin's talk and replied that

no guru or yogi was going to tell me what to do with my life.

'Crikey, you've got a Western ego. You can't do it yourself. You've got to get direction from a real guru, from one who's truly enlightened.'

'But what do you mean by enlightened and how on earth do you tell who's enlightened,' I protested, remembering my previous conviction that Sai Baba was the *avatar*, the only incarnation of God on this planet at this time. I still hadn't quite got over the way I had been so gullible, so blind, to have got caught up in that crazy cult.

'Shut up, someone's coming,' Martin muttered. I kicked the dust with my rubber sandal and glanced up. Down the path walked a figure dressed in a long, white robe. He had his hair tied behind him. He seemed to be walking very carefully and there was a grace about his walk. As he neared us, his face lit up with a smile. I expected to see that his eyes would be glazed with an inward-turned, distant look, but was surprised by their sharpness and clarity.

On reaching the other side of the gate, he said, 'Hari Om' as he placed his hands in prayer position in front of his forehead. Martin gave what I thought was a rather dramatic bow but I could only bring myself to nod my head. As the man worked with several large locks on the gate he looked at me quickly and then turned his attention to the task on hand. 'Swamiji wants to see you too'. I was stunned and asked how the swami could have known I was here. 'Swamiji knows everything.' The man looked directly into my eyes.

As I looked at him, a strange feeling came over me. He was different from what I remembered of the Sai Baba devotees: there was a clarity and a centeredness about him. A gentle power. He didn't look drugged or mesmerized at all. I was intrigued and wondered whether Martin was right about these people after all. I looked at Martin and winked. He grinned at me and I followed him through the gate. Inside the ashram grounds there were masses of flowers growing alongside the path and blanketing the ridges above. Orange and blue birds of paradise flowers thrust out over thick ground covers of small white and orange flowers. The trees and bushes seemed greener here than the vegetation we had passed on our walk up.

The path up to the ashram was very steep and looped around several corners. All the way up we passed beautiful flowering plants and bushes. The ashram buildings were still hidden from sight. At some corners I glanced down and saw the Ganges rushing below us and in the distance I could see the Laxman Jhula Bridge and the few temples nestled on the banks at each end. The view enchanted me. I could hear Martin puffing and gasping in front of me. Finally he stopped and wiped his forehead with his hand, 'I'm going to rest for a few moments. This climb is killing me. Isn't it something?' He waved his hand around expansively.

We stood there together and looked down the valley. Almost directly below us the Ganges formed a rapid as it poured through two sharp bends, banking around the first bend to crash down a steep wall of boulders. The sound coming from this rapid was a constant roar. But there was something quite different about the roaring sound of this mighty river compared to the rivers I had listened to back in New Zealand, some of which were even wider and more torrential. I felt there was something special about the Ganges below me. What it was I could not fathom.

Taking in a deep breath of the cool mountain air, I looked around and noticed that the figure in white had not waited for us and had disappeared around the bend ahead. We resumed our walk and within moments we passed two flagpoles with their orange flags waving gently in the slight breeze. Ahead of us I caught sight of a long stuccoed building, which had a room perched on top. At right angles was another smaller building that seemed to be divided into three rooms as there were three doors opening outwards. I walked closer to the main building and across the wall was painted three sentences in both English and Hindi: 'Lead us from Darkness to Light', 'Lead us from Unreality to Reality' and 'Lead us from Ignorance to Truth'.

Martin stopped at a large concrete water tank, which had a tap near to the ground. He removed his sandals and began to wash his feet and his hands. He gestured at me to do the same. He then walked up to the main building holding his sandals in his left hand. I followed him and we sat down at a bench near the door, dropping our footwear alongside several other pairs of shoes that had been placed nearby. I could not see inside as a thick curtain had been drawn across. The front of the building looked as if it was a partly enclosed veranda, because the front wall was just made of open mesh. I looked around but there was no one in sight. I could hear no sounds coming from inside either. Martin was sitting there with his head thrust back, his eyes closed. I could smell incense wafting out towards us. I could also smell burning eucalyptus leaves that left a clean, fresh sensation in my nose and head.

After some time a voice called softly, 'Come inside, Martin and friend.' I followed Martin as he pulled across the curtain covering the door and stepped inside. At one end of the veranda was a *puja* place set right across the width of the room. This place was ornately decorated with flowers, pictures of Hindu deities and various incense- and candle-holders most of which had candles and incense sticks burning in them. There was a large, white statue of Shiva in one corner and in the opposite corner was a statue of Krishna standing on one leg playing a flute. Behind, resting on the back wall were two large, framed pictures of Shiva, Krishna, and the sage and founder of the *sannyas* tradition, Shankaracharya.

Sitting on the floor in front of the *puja* place was the swami, dressed in a brilliant orange robe. His legs could not be seen, but from the erectness of his back and the position of his knees, I assumed he was sitting in a full lotus position. My first impression was that he looked like a child of twelve or thirteen years, but as I moved closer to take a seat on the floor in front of him, I noticed he could have been anything between twenty and forty years.

He had long, black, shiny hair that flowed well below his shoulders and looked as though it had just been brushed. He had a thin, rather straggly beard and a moustache that was reasonably thick above his lip but which hung in thin strands down the sides of his mouth. Almost at the same time I noticed this moustache, the swami lifted one hand and began twigging one side of it and twirled it upwards. He then proceeded to do the same with the other side and then I noticed that the initial droop of the moustache had gone. On his forehead there was an unusual red *tilak* sign, the shape of a flame with a dot underneath, which stretched from between his eyebrows right up to the hairline. His skin was paler than the average Indian's and his features were very fine. He was extraordinarily beautiful and I couldn't stop staring at him.

As I sat down he smiled at me. I smiled back. He then turned to Martin and spoke clearly in impeccable English. 'Have you decided what you want to do?' Martin put his hands together in a prayer position in front of his chest and answered in a pleading tone, 'I just want to stay here with you, Swamiji. I want to serve you and learn from you.'

I noticed the swami stiffen and his face reddened slightly. He shouted, 'I've told you before. You're not ready to live here. It's very difficult to live here. You have to be ready to die. Yogic *sadhana* is a death of the mind and the ego. Your mind is still very attached to the latrine of the world.'

The swami's use of the word latrine made me gasp inwardly. Martin leapt up and ran to the back of the veranda with his hands clutching onto the sides of his head. He turned and his face was full of anguish. 'Okay, then! I'll go and jump off the Laxman Jhula Bridge.'

Without prostrating or asking for leave of the swami, he ran through the door. The swami yelled in a high pitched voice, 'Jorgen, follow that man.'

I wondered whether I should go after him as well but the swami looked at me and I noticed he wasn't angry anymore. He began to laugh loudly. 'You see what drugs do to the Western brain. Now you don't look as if you've played with drugs. Would you like to live here? We have a three-month introductory course. Preliminary. But most people don't last that long. They get dragged back into the ocean of the world. *Samsara*. I think you are very tired of the world and of your life, are you not?'

I burst into tears. I could not stop them. I felt a piercing pain in my heart. As this dreadful sorrow came over me, I cried and cried burying my head in my hands. Once I glanced upwards and through the streaming water veiling my eyes, I could see the swami sitting there with his eyes closed. I was sure I could see a shining light radiating from his forehead. I buried my head in my hands and continued to weep uncontrollably.

After a time the tears seemed to fade and I felt wonderfully refreshed, I didn't feel drained as I usually felt whenever I had cried in the past for long periods. I looked up to see the swami smiling sweetly at me. I whispered silently to myself, 'He's so beautiful. He's the most beautiful being I've ever laid eyes on.' For a moment I thought I recognized him: that I had known him before. As I glanced over at the clock on the *puja* place I realized I had been sitting there in front of him for over an hour and yet I had no inclination to move from my position even though I was sitting on the bare concrete floor. The swami smoothed out the folds of his gown and placed his hands, palms upright on his knees. 'Too much intellect, that's your problem. That's your real enemy in life. You think too much. Your thoughts leap here and there, create doubts and destroy your faith in the divine.'

Jorgen came to the door with the news that he had not been able to catch up with Martin. The swami yelled at him, 'You big *kudabox*. Go to the Kriya Room and put a bucket of water on your head. That might wake you up.'

He turned to me and winked. I was amazed. It was as if he could turn on and off his anger at will, as if he was in complete control of his emotions. 'Saraswati will give you an application form and a list of things you will need to purchase from Rishikesh for your stay here. Go now.'

Bowing clumsily, I walked out. Standing outside the door was a girl, presumably Saraswati, who handed me some pieces of paper. She too was dressed in white and had frizzy hair sticking up all around her head. Her skin was very pale and she had large saucer-like eyes that seemed to project out of her head as if they were popping out. She turned and walked away without saying a word to me.

As I walked down the path, I thought how strange this place was and how extraordinary it was that the swami had presumed I would come and stay here. I felt a lightness as I wandered slowly down the hill. I was aware of my face feeling soft, as if a deep tension had left it. A glance down at my floral skirt dragging on the ground made me decide to have some white robes made up by a tailor in Rishikesh that afternoon even though the swami had not mentioned any requirements of dress there.

On reaching the downside gate I heard a rustle in the bushes. It was Martin looking very sorry for himself. There was a redness around his eyes, which made me suspect he had been crying. 'You know, it's not fair. This is the only place I've ever wanted to stay at in India. I just don't understand it at all.'

I tried to reassure him and, as we walked down to the Ganges, I gently broke the news to him that I had been invited to stay there. I suggested that perhaps the swami might change his mind about him staying. Perhaps he should be patient and return after a few days.

On the other side of the bridge, we caught a horse *tonga* to Rishikesh. When we reached the market place, Martin left to buy some hashish. I didn't try to change his mind.

A tailor took less than half an hour to sew up two white robes and I left some more material with him to make some more the following day. As he hardly spoke any English, it took me a few minutes to mime and mouth what I wanted him to do. It amazed me to watch him at work. He hardly looked at what he was doing. He sat there on the side of the road with one of those old treadle sewing machines that you work with your feet. The cotton often snapped and I noticed that he never tied up a thread if it broke or at the beginning and end of seams. I had visions of my robes falling apart after a few days. The tailor puffed *beedi* cigarettes continuously and even when the ash dropped on to the new cotton cloth, he did not stop. Only when the seam was finished did he pause, take the cigarette out of his mouth and blow away the ash.

All around him while he worked, children darted in and out, mangy dogs roamed sniffing the ground, men and young boys rode past on old bicycles the wheels of which flung dust in our direction, and groups of men or women moved to and fro. The tailor closely watched everything going on around him. Yet by the time he had finished, he had made two gowns, which, after trying them on over my clothes, were a perfect fit. He had used no pattern, had quickly measured me up beforehand and had not even written down these measurements. The gowns were loose, which is how I wanted them. I was thrilled, especially when he asked for only three rupees for payment. I *namasted* and walked away with the bundle under my arm.

It took a few more hours to purchase the items on the list Saraswati had given me. Most of these were equipment for use in the performing of yogic *kriyas* that I had read about briefly at the Henderson Yoga Ashram. These included a brass vessel with a long spout used for pouring water down one's nostrils and a long bandage cloth that I assumed was for an exercise involving cleaning out the stomach, the thought of which disgusted me. I also purchased two buckets, some straw mats, candles and matches, a torch, a thin mattress called a *resai* and an Indian style broom that was a bunch of straw tied at one end. Laden with these things, I returned to the Tourist Bungalow.

That night as I sat on the veranda outside my room, I filled in the application form I had been given at the ashram. Alongside the question, 'Why do you want to come and stay here?' I wrote, 'I want to find out who I am and what is the meaning of life. I want to find out the truths behind this universe.' As well as questions on previous experience in yoga and meditation, there were other questions requiring details of such things as passport number, place and date of birth.

Martin returned at seven o'clock. He was puffing on a *beedi* cigarette and looked disoriented. I suggested that we go down to a restaurant in the village for a meal. At the restaurant we met up with another Australian, Tom, who was living in a small community of other Westerners and naked Indian *sadhus* (Hindu 'holy' men) on the banks of the Ganges. They had built small grass huts to sleep in and apparently spent most of the time smoking ganja and hashish. I noticed festering sores on his legs and his clothes were dirty and stained. He was a quiet and softly spoken person and, apart from his drug addiction, I thought his company might distract Martin from wallowing in the swami's rejection. The two were soon involved in a conversation together but I did not listen to them. My thoughts were farther away as I imagined what life might be like up on the hill with that strange yogi.

'Wake up, dreamy.' I felt Martin's elbow prod my hip. He turned to the other man. 'She's fallen in love with this yogi.' They both laughed. Tom thumped the table and rolled his eyes, 'Which one is it this time? Not the swami on the other side of the river? Balyogi Premvarni?' Martin nodded. 'Oh, no! You're kidding. That guy's a leech. He's just after money and power and he sleeps with the sheilas. He's dangerous, that one.' Martin protested: 'Don't be ridiculous. He's for real, this one. A true yogi.'

I didn't say anything. I thought to myself that what Tom had passed on was just idle gossip. I felt too excited to entertain doubts.

After the meal I walked back to the Tourist Bungalow by myself as the men wanted to go down by the river and smoke. As I walked away from them I decided not to have anything to do with such people any more. The sooner I got away from hippies and other worldly people and even this dusty, noisy town and up onto that peaceful little hill, the better. I wanted to live a monastic life now — a life of self-control and purity.

ॐ *Chapter 5*

The World on the Hill

And so I entered the world of the 'boy-yogi', as he was known in the district. Life there was simple and rugged and at times strange things went on.

At the beginning, there were three boys and two girls besides me. The male residents were referred to as boys, which seemed to be absurd, if not demeaning, because they were all in their late twenties. Similarly, the female residents were called girls.

Saraswati had lived there the longest. She took me under her wing, so to speak, and told me how I should behave and what to avoid. She originally came from New York, where she had been a drug addict for many years before travelling to India. On the beaches of Goa, on the southeast coast of India, she had heard a story from a fellow traveller that there was a yogi in the Himalayas who could give devotees cosmic experiences without the use of drugs.

Saraswati had large, clear blue eyes and her eyeballs bulged outwards. Because she had developed the habit of blinking infrequently, probably from long periods of gazing at pictures of Lord Shiva, she often had a slightly maniacal look about her.

Her light brown hair was frizzy and stuck out in all directions. Scars from past acne were discernible on her pale face. Even though she treated me like a younger sister and I sometimes felt intimidated by her, she fascinated me. At times I even thought there was an unusual beauty about her.

She was convinced that she would stay here with Swamiji for the rest of her life. On the first day she told me, 'If only you knew who Swamiji is, it would completely blow your mind. There's nobody on this planet working at his level of consciousness. He's put me in touch with my Beloved, my Lord Shiva.' She sighed and leant her head back, and her mouth opened slightly. The irises of her eyes rolled back so only the whites could be seen.

Mariana was altogether different from Saraswati. She was more earthy and worldly. Evidently she was recognised as a talented artist back in Australia. Her brown hair, reaching down her back, was so long that she could almost sit on it. From her nose sparkled a small red ruby stone. She had had her nose pierced by a roadside pedlar in Bombay who had used a rusty piece of wire to dig the hole for it and around the stone you could still see scars from the infections she had developed afterwards.

Swamiji told me Mariana had been a hippy when she had first arrived two months ago, but he claimed that, already, her face was changing; her eyes were clearer and her face was looking purer. But Mariana hardly talked to me; she seemed completely preoccupied. At first I thought she was absorbed in contemplation of some Hindu deity or she was chanting a *mantra* silently, but a few weeks later I realized her thoughts were on Swamiji and what went on in his bedroom.

The three boys were Jorgen from Denmark who was tall, gentle and artistic, Angus — a blond, podgy boy from Scotland, and Michel, a rugged but handsome dark-haired Frenchman with a rubicund complexion.

At first I thought Angus might be mentally retarded as he often gazed at Swamiji with his mouth open, drooling, and his eyes wide and staring. When he was spoken to, he sometimes did not respond and the words had to be repeated. He also seemed to carry out tasks as if in slow motion. Whenever Swamiji yelled at him and called him *kudabox*, he grinned. I later discovered that this word meant idiot. But Angus adored Swamiji. Swamiji said that Angus had more faith than all of the rest of us put together and if he asked him to go and jump off the Laxman Jhula Bridge, he would most likely do so. That was certainly one thing I would never do.

Jorgen had long hair usually tied up in a ponytail. He wore long cream or white robes whereas Angus and Michel usually wore Indian style pajamas. With his long robes and hair, Jorgen had an ethereal look enhanced by his soft voice and graceful movements.

In contrast Michel was often clumsy, like Angus, and his hair was cropped short and he too would grin at (what seemed to me) inappropriate times. As he was strong and muscular, Swamiji often sent him down to the bazaar to collect heavy sacks of flour, rice, or lentils. He was the sort of person who would have looked quite at home on an Australian outback station rather than in this unworldly, spiritual abode. But in spite of his rugged nature, he was surprisingly obedient and servile towards Swamiji.

The boys had been given *Sanskrit* names but they

were seldom used except in front of Indian visitors. Mariana was sometimes called Sangam, which meant confluence, but Saraswati was called mostly by this name, the name of the Hindu goddess of wisdom, and not her American name, Randy.

There was a third set of names that only Swamiji used, especially when we were carrying out assigned work with varying degrees of resistance. Saraswati would be called the fox, as Swamiji said she was sly and cunning like most Americans. Michel was called the pig because he was obsessed with food and often farted during *satsang* times. Jorgen was the dog because, as Swamiji pointed out, he liked to run around in circles, barking uselessly. (The dog is not generally kept as a pet in India as they are usually rabies carriers and are thin and mangy-looking.) Mariana's special name was the cat. Swamiji explained that if you stroke her gently she responds in a friendly way but if she is threatened or upset she flares up and scratches.

After a few days Swamiji began calling me the mouse. That really annoyed me because I didn't want to be seen as timid or scuttling here and there! Swamiji reckoned that many New Zealanders have the characteristics of mice and it had something to do with the geographical location and size of the country.

When Swamiji used these animal names it was if he was sneering at us, as if he was mirroring something about ourselves that we did not want to acknowledge. I often called Swamiji Leo the lion but not to his face. As it was, his astrological sign was Leo, ruler of the jungle: the same sign as my father's. But sometimes Swamiji's changing moods reminded me more of a chameleon.

I was surprised how easy it was to settle into the general routine of life at this ashram. For many years I had become accustomed to doing virtually what I pleased. Here there were many rules and regulations as well as a rigid timetable to be followed.

Each morning Swamiji woke us up at 4.30 a.m. by blowing on a conch, the noise of which could be heard even at the other side of the property or down at the gate half a kilometre away. Fortunately for most of my life I had been an early riser and at university had usually done most of my study in the early hours of the morning, so getting up at this time did not disturb me at all. The first thing we did was to bathe and carry out our *kriyas* before assembling at 5 a.m. on the front veranda of the main building for *satsang*. Here we would meditate and chant *Vedic* prayers and also read out aloud passages from the *Bhagavad Gita*, the *Shiva Puranas*, the *Yog Vashishta* or the *Ramayana*. Most days Swamiji would give an impromptu talk about some aspect of the mind and consciousness, the 'science of the soul' as he called it.

When *satsang* had finished, *chai* was prepared. A mixture of spices such as ginger, cloves, cardamom and cinnamon were boiled in water for a few minutes and then tea-leaves, sugar and milk added and then brought to the boil. We drank this *chai* from tall stainless steel tumblers (without handles) that for some reason were called 'glasses' in the ashram. To avoid getting our hands burnt, we had to gingerly grip the top of these glasses with the tips of our fingers. The *chai* made at the ashram was delicious and sometimes during *satsang* I found myself hoping that it would finish soon so *chai* could be prepared. This was the only food or drink (apart from water) permitted before lunchtime.

After *chai* time we spent a few hours doing various chores around the ashram. Cleaning and sweeping (especially the main veranda and Swamiji's rooms downstairs and upstairs) were our major tasks. I enjoyed these jobs even though in the past I considered such work dreary and menial. It was also good to be busy as for the past few months I seemed to have spent a lot of time lounging around with not enough to occupy myself.

Jorgen was the only boy allowed to clean the veranda — Swamiji said the other two were too clumsy and rough. Jorgen was evidently adept with his hands in many areas including drawing and painting and was also excellent at sewing and mending and was sometimes given the task of mending or altering Swamiji's robes.

During the first few weeks one of my many jobs was cleaning the veranda with Jorgen. As well as taking out all the mats and shaking them thoroughly, occasionally we would haul them up onto the roof to air. Then we would sweep and wash the floor using rags and cold water. Apart from the floor area, we had to dust and clean the shelves and the objects placed on them. Particular attention was paid to the *puja* place. After it was thoroughly dusted and cleaned, objects would be rearranged on it and sometimes pictures were replaced. Flowers that had dropped from plants and shrubs would be collected and arranged around the statues of deities or made into garlands and hung around the pictures. Fresh incense would be placed in their brass holders. New candles would replace the sunken blobs that remained from the morning *satsang* or the night before.

After a few days Swamiji allocated the job of

cleaning and rearranging the *puja* place (our place of worship) to me alone, as he said it was apparent that I had an affinity with this area. Even though such tasks and rituals were quite new to me, this soon became my favourite work.

Saraswati usually prepared most of the food and sometimes Mariana assisted her. Swamiji always supervised. The boys were not allowed to cook or prepare food as Swamiji said they would poison the food with their greed. But they sometimes worked in or near the kitchen as their jobs included collecting wood and charcoal for the kitchen fire, and collecting heavy buckets of water from the water tank. Several buckets of water were left in a row outside the door and used for either washing dishes of for food preparation. The kitchen was a very small, dark room with no windows. The floor and the benches were covered with packed cow dung. There was no fridge.

We had little freedom with food in the ashram. Swamiji oversaw not only the preparation but also the serving of it into small *catoris* on stainless steel *thalis*. We were never allowed to eat food except at designated mealtimes. The only substantial meal was at midday and at night we had a small snack and sometimes just fruit or soup. But I noticed that most mornings Swamiji would go into the kitchen and prepare for himself a *catori* of food. At mealtimes he was prepared a special *thali* and was often given delicacies that were not served to the aspirants.

Some of the other chores assigned to the boys were filling buckets of water and leaving them inside the toilets. When we used the toilet we would flush them by hurling a bucket or two of water into the bowl. The boys also swept and washed out the Kriya Room, cleaned down the toilets and washed Swamiji's clothes and bed linen.

It soon became apparent to me though that the boys' favourite job was the purchasing of provisions from the market place at Swargashram or further away at Rishikesh. Swargashram was the name given to a cluster of temples, ashrams, *kutirs* (cottages) and shops on this side of the river almost opposite the large Shivananda Ashram. It was from Swargashram that boats travelled across the Ganges to the steps of the Shivananda Ashram.

Most mornings were spent constantly working but Swamiji explained that work was our yoga *sadhana* as well and even more important than doing yoga *asanas* or *pranayama* exercises. His explanation was that working and serving the guru was *karma* yoga and facilitates the purification of the ego to a greater extent than other branches of yoga.

In the afternoon, after a lunch consisting usually of rice, *chapattis*, spiced vegetables and curd, there was a rest period when Swamiji usually locked himself in one of his bedrooms. At two o'clock the downside gate was opened for visitors. During visiting time we were expected to keep out of sight unless called upon and we were not allowed to leave the ashram without Swamiji's permission. One of the boys would be assigned the duty of looking after visitors when they arrived. If they were Western visitors they usually had to be reminded to wash their feet before being seated on one of the benches near the veranda; they would then be offered a glass of water from the Ganges. The boy on duty had to stay nearby in case Swamiji or a visitor needed anything.

I spent this spare time at the back of the Kriya Room writing letters home, washing my clothes or reading. Some days I was given permission to go for a walk through the jungle or down to the Ganges. About five o'clock, after the last of the visitors had left, we usually met on the veranda for another *satsang*. When this *satsang* was over, a light supper was prepared, usually a piece of fruit or drink. Even though I found myself beginning to think more about food, seldom did I feel hungry.

At night the boys slept in the Kriya Room. I presumed Saraswati slept in her own room and Mariana slept in the cottage behind the main building called the Shakti Kutir. For the first few weeks I slept up on the Kriya Room roof on a straw mat, but at some time during the night I would usually be woken by rain splashing on my face. I would then scramble down to a corner of the musty Kriya Room and spend the rest of the night there. Sometimes, if it was only a slight rain, I stayed up on the roof because my sleeping bag was waterproof. I loved it up on the roof and the noise from the Ganges seemed much louder up there and even the stars seemed brighter and closer.

Before I went to sleep each night, Swamiji would walk up the steps to the Kriya Room roof and walk over to me. I would be already outstretched on my thin straw mat and gazing up at the canopy of stars far above me. He would stand there and stroke my feet with his toes. Once he said: 'Beautiful galaxy is it not? Everything is dancing. The moon is dancing. The jungle is dancing. Ganga is dancing. The dance of life.' He would then turn and walk away with his orange robe trailing behind him. My heart moved to hear such words. I often felt completely mesmerized by him and overcome by his power and his beauty.

This magical environment enchanted me: it was a place of sheer beauty. Apart from the natural beauty of the untouched jungle, within the ashram itself foreign and native flower seeds had been planted and in spite of the sudden and dramatic changes in weather, things grew here and flourished in an extraordinary, almost unnatural way.

As for the buildings in the ashram, they were unlike anything I had ever lived in.

For the first few months I had no room or space to call my own and stored my possessions in the Kriya Room. This Kriya Room, where most of the *kriyas* were performed, was a large, gloomy room, which ran across the back of the storeroom, the kitchen and Saraswati's room. Inside this room was an open area for bathing with a hole in the outside wall for the water to run out. Our baths were taken squatting down using a plastic jug and a bucket of cold water. At the back of the Kriya Room were rows and rows of shelves full of *kriya* equipment. The boys also stored their possessions there — sleeping bags, clothing, mats and such things. About a third of the outer wall of the room was open, with a large, mildewed tarpaulin that could be rolled down when it was raining. Running along the outside was a narrow concrete veranda and jutting out from each end were two Indian style toilets. It was out the back here that we washed our clothes by hand and hung them over ropes strung between some guava trees. There was a dreadful, musty smell in the Kriya Room and at times there were other smells during the performing of *kriyas* or from the using of toilets. The room was messy and cluttered and there seemed to be large amounts of junk stored away there. I soon learnt that a lot of this had been left by past students. For some reason I got the impression that they must have wanted to get out of this place as quickly as possible.

There were three rooms on the other side of this building. These rooms as well as the Kriya Room had no internal access to each other and could only be entered through their external doors. There was the storeroom, in which foodstuffs were stored in bulk; the kitchen was in the middle, and on the far end was Saraswati's room (she had paid for the building of this room herself). This room had been extended on to the end of the building, which itself was only a few years old.

Adjacent to this building was the main building of the ashram in which were Swamiji's two bedrooms — one downstairs and the other upstairs. The latter was only accessible by a staircase that ran from one end of the veranda up onto the roof. Outside this room was a sign 'Meditation Room' written in both English and Hindi. In both bedrooms were large beds that were called *cots*. The bases were made of solid wood with no slats or springs. This meant that several times a week we would have to drag the many *resais*, which together served as a mattress, up onto the flat roof to air. This was essential during the rainy season as clothing and bedding quickly became damp and mildewed. I often wished that Swamiji could have just slept on a straw mat or a single *resai* like the rest of us because the lifting of these heavy *resais* became a tedious chore. From my first day, I often wondered why Swamiji lived in relative comfort while we aspirants endured discomforts.

It was not only the encroaching jungle that invited dampness, but also the roughness of the buildings. There were gaps under and on top of all the doors and windows where the wind and rain sometimes entered. There were few straight lines anywhere. Even the roof undulated at various places and so when it rained, water would collect in large puddles, which we had to sweep over the side with thick straw brooms. The unevenness in the buildings somehow added to their character.

There were many things about this environment I was finding odd and eccentric and this appealed to me. My flight to India was in a way a rebellion against all that was conventional, sociable and normal and I was slowly beginning to realize that there were things about my father to admire. He was scrupulously honest in many ways and was very direct with people. He said exactly what he thought, which made most people feel quite uncomfortable around him. It was becoming more and more evident to me that conventional and happy people seem to live rather uninteresting and dull lives.

In each of Swamiji's rooms was an *almari*, a large cupboard. Swamiji's many clothes – robes, shawls, jumpers and other items – were neatly folded on several shelves. Inside the *almari* in the downstairs room was also a large, heavy safe in which were stored the passports and valuables of residents. This safe was kept locked by two large padlocks at the top and the bottom. Locks were present in every door and virtually every cupboard or *almari* in the ashram. Indians in general seemed to have a fetish about locks and keys.

No outsiders were allowed into either of Swamiji's two bedrooms and the boys were allowed in only on very rare occasions. At first I could not understand this exclusion but I was too fearful of Swamiji's apparent displays of wrath to question him about it. During my first week there Saraswati had cautioned me. 'We don't talk unnecessarily here. Nor should we ask Swamiji questions. When you learn to accept Swamiji as your guru you will understand what is going on here'. She spoke softly, with little trace of the harsh American accent of so many of her compatriots, and when she spoke I sensed a power, an authority behind her words. Even though I thought she was strange, I also held her in awe. She seemed more 'advanced' than the others.

There were two other rooms in the main building besides Swamiji's two bedrooms and the veranda (which ran right across the front of the building and was like a room in itself because it was about twelve feet wide). One was the office and the other was called the 'cloth room'. The boys were rarely allowed to enter either of these two rooms.

In the cloth room were about eight large trunks of Swamiji's clothes, bed linen, blankets and hand-loomed brightly coloured mats for the floor, pictures and *puja* items. There was also a trunk of clothing left behind by female disciples, some of whom Swamiji had never heard from again. On entering this room for the first time I was appalled by the amount of things stored there, much of which was hardly used. Why didn't Swamiji give some of it away to the lepers living in the colony on the other side of the Laxman Jhula Bridge? Why was he such a hoarder?

The office also was cluttered with things. At least a dozen tape recorders were kept there, as well as some radios, cameras and clocks. In this room were kept all the files of disciples' letters. There were also carbon copies of every letter written to them by Swamiji that he usually dictated to a resident to write by hand. People who had stayed for lengthy periods of time had their own file. I sometimes had the urge to open some of these files to find out what past students thought of Swamiji and perhaps find out why they left. But on my first day at the ashram Swamiji made it quite clear that I was never to touch them without his permission. There were also files of correspondence to government offices arranging visa extensions and bulky files of past bills and accounts.

Two built-in bookcases containing hundreds of books, mostly texts on Hinduism or *Vedanta* philosophy, reached from the floor to the ceiling. In the office was also stored a waterbed (given to Swamiji by an American disciple) that was put away during the rainy season and the winter months. Saraswati explained that during other times of the year Swamiji slept on it upstairs on the roof.

On one occasion when noticing Swamiji was in a 'good mood' I questioned him about all his possessions and why he even asked disciples returning from overseas to bring back certain things for him that he never paid for. He grinned like a little boy: 'I'm just enjoying the *lila*, the divine dance of life. These are just my playthings. I don't need anything on the personal level.' When Swamiji spoke like this (even though I did not know what he meant), I still accepted his explanation. Somehow he seemed to have that effect on all the people here. He spoke with such 'knowingness' and there often seemed to be an enchanting mystery behind the words themselves.

About a week after I had gone there to stay, I awoke early one morning before the conch was sounded. I glanced over to the main building and caught sight of Saraswati, white gown fluttering. She moved out of Swamiji's upstairs room and darted across the roof and down the internal steps into the veranda. A few seconds later I could hear the grating of the bolt on the inside door and then she slipped out and ran quickly across to her room.

I sat there with doubts beginning to invade the peace of my mind, wondering whether she had been sleeping with Swamiji. I felt disgusted at the possibility because swamis were meant to be celibate. Not only that, in daily lectures Swamiji had preached the necessity of being celibate to maintain a strict yogic way of life. I had only just recovered from the shock of discovering that Sai Baba enjoyed sex in unconventional ways. Surely this yogi was not feigning piety also? Only the day before, Swamiji had read from the *Bhagavad Gita*, Lord Krishna's explanation to the warrior Arjuna, 'With the self calmed and free from fear, firm in the vow of celibacy, having controlled the mind, let him sit harmonized, his thoughts on Me, absorbed in Me.' I felt shattered.

During morning *satsang* when Swamiji spoke about Realisation and the 'awakening of one's real self', I felt myself cringing inside. I was too frightened to confront him directly with my suspicions but instead began to ask him questions, requesting definitions for the terms he was using. My voice sounded nasty and twisted. Swamiji was sitting in a full lotus position in front of us. His look pierced me. 'An academic brain. You won't understand anything with that intellect of yours. First you must learn not to question. When you accept me as your guru, like the others here, then you will begin to understand. You have to earn the guru's knowledge through his grace. Learn to surrender. I know everything that goes on here, everything in your petty, grasping minds. These doubts of yours. You think I'm sleeping with the girls, don't you?

I didn't say anything but felt myself blushing and looked down, ashamed. I wanted to run away and hide somewhere. He could see through me; somehow he could read my thoughts, look into my mind! I was completely taken aback. Even though I felt foolish and slightly fearful that he could actually read my mind, yet this also convinced me that he was an extraordinary, superhuman person after all. No wonder the others here were so devoted and servile to him.

I decided to conquer this doubting mind of mine and put my full attention on what I had come here for: to learn hatha and other types of yoga and live in a disciplined environment. I became determined to master all the *kriyas* — the one thing I had not looked forward to before beginning this yogic way of life. In fact I had dreaded them. Fortunately, Guruji, back at the Henderson Yoga Ashram in Auckland, had described these *kriyas* to me so at least I was psychologically partly prepared for what I had to try to master.

Within the first hour of walking up the path to begin my stay at the ashram, Saraswati had introduced me to the first *kriya*, the *neti kriya*. This involved the use of a brass container, a *neti lota*, filled with warm, salty water. From one end of this container was a long, narrow spout, which was for inserting up one nostril at a time. With the head tilted at the correct angle, the water was supposed to flow right up that nostril and down through the other nostril. I was expecting it to be painful, but was surprised that it only produced a tingling sensation at the top of my nostrils and I was sure I could breathe more easily afterwards.

But this was the easiest of the *kriyas*. The ones that followed were more difficult and at first I found them rather repugnant. I learnt to twist a thin rubber tube up either nostril and push it downwards through my throat so as to cleanse the nasal passages. My first attempt at this variation of the *neti kriya* brought sharp pains, because the tube was grating along raw, previously untouched flesh. But I persisted and on subsequent occasions it was easier to do and only slightly unpleasant.

I was also taught the *kunjal kriya*, which in effect was nothing more than induced vomiting. This involved the rapid drinking of about half a bucket of warm salted water and then moving the abdominal muscles and organs laterally and vertically in a surging motion (a hatha yoga exercise called *nauli*). The aim of this *kriya* was to force the contents of the stomach up and out of the mouth in one or several whooshes. At first I was expecting a bitter, putrid taste in my mouth as from vomiting but as this *kriya* is done early in the morning before one eats or drinks anything the only thing that is regurgitated is the salted water along with what Saraswati described as 'excess mucus'. I felt surprisingly refreshed after my first attempt at this *kriya* and it was one of the few I decided to practise on a regular basis.

Lastly, after some initial resistance, I managed to swallow yards upon yards of white bandage-like cloth into my stomach and regurgitate it again. This *kriya* was considered more effective than the *kunjal kriya* but after mastering it, I seldom repeated it. Unlike the *kunjal kriya*, no water was drunk to help expel any residual mucus and I was slightly revolted by the retching motions produced from the irritation of the cloth being forced down my oesophagus. I also began to wonder how necessary this 'elimination of mucus' was. Perhaps mucus was meant to be there as a natural secretion of the stomach.

After two weeks there was only one *kriya* I had not practised, and in spite of my renewed determination to make the most of my stay here, the more I heard about it, the less I wanted to do it. This was the *varishar kriya* and involved washing out the whole intestinal tract right through to the rectum and anus. The *kriya* takes several hours to complete successfully and involves rapidly drinking buckets of salted water and performing special *asanas* vigorously. But we were not allowed to try this *kriya* until we had spent two months in the ashram. The reasoning behind this was that we needed to wait until our bodies had purified themselves to a certain extent.

Even though the first few weeks were relatively peaceful (on account of the quality of the physical environment more than anything else), at least several times a day as I watched Swamiji in action and saw his moods change suddenly and dramatically, I felt disturbed and wondered whether I had made the right decision in coming here to stay after all. Swamiji was so much in control here. We were not allowed to question anything he said or did. This frightened me and brought back memories of living with my father for he too had been like this. But most of the time Swamiji was gentle and almost playful with us during *satsang* times. He sometimes looked like a wise old man benevolent and all-knowing.

Mariana was the only aspirant who sometimes stood up to him, argued and questioned him. Sometimes Swamiji would laugh at her confrontations. At other times he would get angry with her and she would get enraged and usually storm around to the Shakti Kutir. But the other aspirants hardly raised their voice to Swamiji and were very obedient. They seemed to worship him but I never knew what was going on in their minds and what they sometimes thought of Swamiji.

I had only been at the ashram for about three weeks when Saraswati approached me. 'Swamiji wants to see you in the downstairs bedroom.' She looked slightly flustered. Then, without waiting for my reply, she rushed past me into her room and slammed the doors shut. I could hear her locking the door inside by the sound of the long metal bolt grating. She then banged the shutters of the window and bolted these as well. I thought how weird this place sometimes was. At times people here seemed to be so emotional and behaved like little children as they ran here and there, sometimes crying and sometimes shouting. Yet at other times they seemed so much in control, detached and almost glowing, like a superior race of human beings. Swamiji, at the centre of it all, was the weirdest.

I walked towards the veranda door and noticed the heavy curtains were drawn right across. I opened then slightly and called, 'Did you want to see me Swamiji?' He answered softly, 'Yes.' Bolt the veranda door and come in here.'

When I walked into his room it was in darkness except for a candle burning in the outer window alcove. There were two small windows in the room. One opened out to the outside and the other opened onto the veranda. On two of the walls were large, framed pictures of the gods Krishna and Shiva. These pictures were quite extraordinary and seemed very old. They were not at all like the pictures of Hindu deities available in the market place. Those are shiny and crass and the gods depicted look like movie stars rather than ethereal beings. In the outer window alcove were arranged some smaller pictures as well as photos of past female disciples. There were also several incense and candleholders. A candle was alight as well as several sandalwood sticks from which coils and whirls of pleasant smelling smoke drifted throughout the room. Even though the room was sparsely furnished, it was a beautiful room. It was so peaceful inside and quite different from the other rooms in the ashram.

Swamiji was lying on his cot with his back to the wall and his head supported by one hand. The bright orange colour of both his loose robe and the curtains hanging down over the window blazed in the semi-darkness. I knelt down on the mat on the floor alongside his bed. Swamiji patted the space alongside him, 'Come and sit here'.

I stood up and sat on the edge of the bed. I felt uncomfortable about being on the same level as he was. It seemed to me to be somewhat improper but I wondered whether perhaps he was about to bestow on me an aspirant name in *Sanskrit* or perhaps a secret *mantra* to use in my meditation.

He looked intently at me and I wondered what he was 'picking up' from my mind. His free arm was resting loosely along the side of his body, down the valley of his waist and up over his slim hips. He looked like the reclining Buddha but his face was like that of the boy Krishna. I still couldn't get used to the fact that he was a man, as he sometimes seemed to me so androgynous: a fusion of female beauty and masculine strength and power. He smiled at me seductively, 'How do you like it here?'

I put my head down and I could feel my cheeks burning. 'It's wonderful, Swamiji,' I murmured. Suddenly he reached over and pulled me down on the cot and began kissing me. His tongue began to push his saliva into my mouth. Stunned, I just lay there rigid like a corpse and before I knew it he had pulled up my robe, manoeuvred his penis between my legs and was inside me. But I did not resist him. There was no roughness or jerkiness about his movements. It was if I was floating into him. His skin felt like the softest silk and the touch of his body sliding up and down gently on top of me was like liquid. It was as if I was being moved and caressed by the waves of an ocean, an ocean not of water, but of a thicker, jelly-like substance. But I felt no sexual arousal. Even though I was acutely aware of the unusual softness of his skin, I was scarcely aware of our sexual organs connecting nor was I aware of any other physical sensations. But I could feel my heart opening and feelings of love flooding me. I kept feeling as if my mind and my consciousness of who I was were drifting away from me.

I was jolted back to the physical reality of the situation when I heard a pitiful sound come from his mouth. Seconds later I looked down to see he was mopping himself with his scarf, which he then handed to me. 'Dry yourself. Just raising your *kundalini*. Now go.'

Swamiji moved off the cot and began to change his robe. He then went to the mirror and began to comb his beard and moustache.

I struggled to get up off the cot but there was a strange dizziness in my head as if I had taken some sort of drug. I groped my way to the door and walked outside into the veranda and out to the garden. I looked up to the mountains towering in the distance and breathed deeply. Dark clouds were moving towards us and there was a stillness in the air. Within the hour we would have a glorious storm with thunder crackling, lightning dancing and the rain pouring onto the Himalayan Hill. Swamiji loved it when there were storms. He showed a child-like rapture as he watched the movement and listened to the sounds outside. This place and this person at the centre of it were magical.

Feeling light and graceful, I walked slowly around to the water tanks near the Shakti Kutir. I laughed to myself. I didn't feel guilty at all. It was a wonderful experience. For months I had been carrying around the idea that to be sincerely spiritual one needed to be celibate. All the books I had been studying had stipulated this requirement. But perhaps they were wrong and I had been mistaken. This unexpected experience had seemed so 'right'.

On reaching the water tanks, I slipped off my robes and slid into the cool water amongst the frogs and the pink lotus flowers. For a long time I lay there with my eyes closed listening to the Ganges roaring in the distance. I felt a strange closeness to that river. I decided from that moment to begin to call her Ganga, my Mother Ganga. Far away beyond

The Serpent Rising

the back wall I could hear the laughter and the singing of some of the village children as they collected sticks and twigs for their earthen stoves.

A few days after my 'initiation', I was washing my clothes at the back of the Kriya Room when Mariana suddenly appeared from behind one of the guava trees. She was wearing what looked like one of Swamiji's old orange robes though it had faded to more of a pink colour. When she saw me she looked startled.

'Don't you think it's rather strange here? What do you think of Swamiji? Is he your guru?' I blurted out. She gave me the kind of look that suggested that I must be incredibly stupid. Her prominent eye-teeth were bared. She snarled at me under her breath: 'I can't talk to you now.'

I couldn't understand why she was so unfriendly to everyone. 'But what do you think about Swamiji sleeping with us?' I assumed he slept with the three of us and that the other two would have known Swamiji had given me my initiation. In fact, I assumed that the boys also would have been aware of what was going on in Swamiji's bedroom.

But a dreadful look crossed her face. I thought she was going to attack me. 'He's sleeping with you! The fucking little bastard.' She began to wave her arms up and down and rushed away.

I began to shake all over and hid in the Kriya Room behind the open door. Mariana began to yell hysterically from the other side of the building. Then there was a loud banging of doors. Swamiji began to shout in a high-pitched voice. 'Get out of this place. Go back to Goa to your drug addicts. You're not ready for yoga *sadhana*. You're too emotional. Angus, go and open the downside gate for her. We don't want people like that here. This is meant to be a place of peace. People like that are destroying me.' I then heard Mariana shouting and screaming and seconds later I could hear heavy footsteps running down the path.

For a long time I hid in the Kriya Room. My heart was beating madly. I felt so overwhelmed with fear I couldn't move. When finally I heard Swamiji calling my name, I walked sheepishly and nervously to the veranda. Swamiji was standing there but he didn't look angry at all. He grinned at me: 'Little mouse been hiding somewhere. Go with Saraswati and she will teach you how to make *elaichi chai*.'

During the evening *satsang* Swamiji gave a talk on 'divine love'. He said that what we thought of as love was just attachment. We were easily bound by jealousy. Love was the pure energy of the divine with no expectations, no attachment. Human beings seldom experience it. What they call love is either lust or possessiveness. He was obviously referring to Mariana but I was still very disturbed by her leaving so suddenly.

The following day Swamiji locked himself in the bedroom and did not come out. Saraswati explained to me that he was contacting Mariana on another level in an attempt to sort out her *karma*.

We never saw Mariana again. Two months later a Westerner, who had met Mariana down at Goa after she had left the ashram, visited Swamiji. He brought with him a newspaper clipping in which there was the shocking news that Mariana had been murdered: the article said she had been caught smuggling hard drugs into Sydney and while out on bail she had gone missing. The police found her body at the bottom of Sydney harbour with an anchor chained around her feet.

I was deeply shaken by this news. But Swamiji seemed quite detached and unaffected. He remarked: 'It's just her *karma*. She had strong *samskaras* that pulled her back into the drug world. But just the short stay that she had here would have lifted the state of her soul. Already she has entered another body. Death is only the passing on to a new life, a fresh start.'

But I had no direct knowledge of reincarnation and I could not understand why Swamiji was not upset. It took me some months to recover from the shock of Mariana's death. I couldn't help blaming myself in some way. Swamiji tried to reassure me by saying she would have left sooner or later. He said I was lucky I had not been involved with drugs and the hippy culture. But he warned me sternly never to talk to anyone again about what went on in his bedroom.

Chapter 6

This 'Teacher of Mine'

So it was that whenever Swamiji called me into his room I was prepared for what would usually follow.

This room as well as the room directly above it, (called the Meditation Room though it was never used for the purpose of meditation), felt very different from other rooms in the ashram. Whenever I entered either of these rooms there was a sense of moving into another world, another place of existence. The air seemed to be charged with intense electrical energy but at the same time there was an atmosphere of deep stillness and prayerfulness — far more so than I had experienced in various churches and cathedrals or even Hindu temples I had visited.

Swamiji spent much of his time in these two rooms, especially the downstairs one, not only at night but also during the day. He seldom used the upstairs room during the rainy season and never used it during mid-winter. The downstairs room was like the vortex of the ashram: the heart of things as well as the central command station. It was from this room that Swamiji would shout (in his high-pitched voice) orders and instructions to residents.

He would shout through the internal window between his room and the veranda — a window covered with grills and dark mesh on the outside and with bright orange curtains on the inside. There were also internal shutters that could be closed as well. It was impossible to see into the room from the veranda unless one was very close up to this window. The foot of Swamiji's cot almost reached this window so he could still call out without leaving his bed.

Swamiji seemed to enjoy lying down. Sometimes he would spend the whole day lying on his cot (on rare occasions, several days) only getting up to go to the toilet or have a quick wash. He claimed to able to meditate from this prone position. Even when lying down with his eyes closed, he claimed to be able to see everything going on in the ashram, as well as anything that was going on in the world at any time. All he had to do was simply focus his attention on a person or place. Swamiji claimed that in reality the ashram was his subtle body and all the rooms reflected parts of that body. Most of the time I was able to accept such explanations without questioning.

In the downstairs room incense was burnt almost continuously and whenever Swamiji was inside at least one candle would be lit. These things, he said, were to frighten away evil spirits.

For the first five months, throughout the rainy season and the beginning of winter, I was called into this room at least once daily, usually more. The procedure was invariably the same. If anyone else was in the veranda area or in either of the two rooms alongside Swamiji's bedroom (the office and the cloth room), that person would be sent away.

The veranda door would then be bolted from the inside and the heavy braid curtains drawn right across. Swamiji's room would be bolted from the inside as well. In that darkened room full of the sweet smell and wispy smoke of incense, Swamiji would lie down first and then pat the space alongside him and beckon me to come and lie with him. I would never lie down first. This was not the ritual of worldly lovemaking, so everything was done at his invitation. We were not lovers. He was the guru and I was the disciple.

In the warm weather he would usually wear only thin cotton shorts or in the cooler weather one of his many robes. I would be asked to take off my white robe, but sometimes he would simply thrust it up out of his way. A few days after my initiation Swamiji suggested that I stop wearing underclothes for he said traditional Indian women never wore such restrictive and unhealthy garments. But later, when I was in a doubting frame of mind, I wondered whether he just didn't want the hassle of pulling them down or asking me to do so before sliding on top of me and quickly entering me. I never once considered resisting his advances, regardless of how I was feeling towards him. This was one less obstruction to his karmic obligation as he called it.

Once I asked him, 'Why do you preach celibacy in your lectures? And why aren't the boys here allowed to have sex?' He laughed. 'This isn't sex. Sex is what you had with your worldly men. I am just raising your *kundalini*.' At times I did feel a sensation like a fiery liquid moving at the base of my spine, at my tailbone, and rising upwards to the top of my head.

Swamiji told me he had no desire for sex. His

'raising of our energy, or *kundalini*', as he put it, was something he did only for our own sakes, to remove deep *samskaras* from our subconscious. To eliminate all the impurities that had penetrated us from years of sleeping with worldly men. He insisted that this was the only *sadhana* I needed here. I believed him because each time we had been together, I felt energised but at the same time my mind became still and peaceful. Swamiji showed no apparent interest in whether I attained physical pleasure or reached orgasm (at least not in the ways I had been used to in my past), but the strangest thing was that even though he was in an out of me very quickly, and there was never any foreplay, afterwards I always felt in an orgasmic state.

Usually at the end, a truly wretched noise came from his mouth. It was not the sound of physical release, but if was as if each act scarred his heart and soul. When I asked him why he made such a sad sound, he would explain that there was so much pain and confusion in our psyches and still so much to clean. He just wanted to go back and rest in his divine nature but he was compelled by a karmic obligation to help his beloved disciples.

After some sessions he gave me a stainless steel *catori* to let any trapped seminal juices seep into the container. I would take this into the kitchen, mix the juices with honey and *malai* (the cream that was skimmed off the milk after it had been boiled) and return to Swamiji. There I was expected to eat the contents in front of him. He called it 'the nectar of the gods' though it tasted simply like thickened honey and cream.

If there were any wet patches on the sheets, Swamiji would mop these up with his thin cotton scarf, usually pausing to sniff it and remark how pure the smell was. When the room was in order, Swamiji would go out to his tiny bathroom poked into the corner of the veranda under the stairwell, rinse out the scarf and leave it in the bucket where his soiled clothes were kept. It was the job of one of the boys or a servant to wash these clothes and I often wondered what they thought of these scarves and the orange sheets they washed and hung to dry on the Kriya Room roof. Not only the scarves, but also all the sheets had numerous stains. Stains from years of sleeping with Western girls.

The sheets, pillowcases and covers of the two beds upstairs and downstairs were orange in colour as was all of Swamiji's clothing. Orange is the colour worn by the Hindu *sannyasin* and is meant to represent the colour of the symbolic fire in which all desires for worldly pleasures are extinguished. The orange and the green colours of the jungle were the only bright colours in this world on the hill as the residents were expected to wear clothes of white or cream. Even the flowers growing in the garden were mostly orange hued.

The orange of Swamiji's clothes was not the dull orange-ochre colour often worn by the *sannyasin* or monk because once a year many of his clothes were dispatched to Rishikesh to be redyed a brilliant orange colour. As well as his faded clothes, many of the stained sheets were sent. But when they were returned the stains were never quite covered or hidden from the dye. What did the *dhobi wallahs* (the washermen); think of all these stains on the sheets of the 'celibate' yogi who lived high on the hill? Swamiji was revered as well as feared in the district because the local people had heard stories of weird things happening in that isolated abode, stories of Westerners running away with looks of terror on their faces. The understanding of some of the villagers was that we were all drug-crazed hippies whom the yogi was trying to help.

Whenever I was alone with Swamiji in his bedroom, my monkey-mind would stop racing and doubting, and I would feel like staying in that room forever — it would be easy to die there. In that room, I sometimes felt as if I had already done everything I wanted to do in my life and wondered whether it was possible for me (or at least my body) to burst into flames and dissolve into light, the fire of love, in the same way that Mira Bai (the famous devotee of Krishna) was supposed to have done centuries ago.

Some weeks after Mariana had run away, I was given permission to use the Shakti Kutir behind the main building and near the high stonewall at the back of the ashram. Outside the door of this tiny *kutir* were two concrete water tanks sunk into the ground. They were seldom drained of water and cleaned, yet still we bathed in them. The tanks were also home to frogs that croaked loudly at night, their sounds echoing around the ashram. They seldom rested on the shiny, green pads of the beautiful lotus flowers growing there, preferring instead the mud and the slime. Swamiji often used to remark on these frogs in his lectures pointing out the parallels with dirty minds and enlightened ones. The mud and slime he likened to the market place and the world outside.

In this *kutir* I kept all my possessions and on one of the shelves at the head of the hard wooden cot I set up my own *puja* place. Swamiji gave me several framed pictures of Hindu deities to hang on the walls.

The only furniture in this one-roomed *kutir* was the cot, which took up most of the space. The walls were roughly plastered and painted sky blue, the floor was concrete with no mat. As there were no windows, and dense foliage crept over one side and onto the roof from the encroaching jungle, it was damp inside with a musty smell so I began to burn incense whenever I was there. I was so glad to have a place to call my own and where I could write letters to my parents and write poems to Swamiji who was gradually becoming my beloved more than my guru.

Some days Swamiji would walk around to the Shakti Kutir especially in the afternoon if there were no visitors. Sometimes he would bolt the door and we would lie down on the cot. At other times he would glance behind him to check whether anyone was watching and he would kiss me, dribbling saliva into my mouth. Or he would stand over me as I sat on the cot and press his body against mine while stroking my head gently.

On one of these visits he brought me a gift of a small marble Shiva *lingam* worshipped throughout India especially in the Shiva temples. As the name suggests, it is simply the shape of an erect penis though this is always resting on a base shaped like a *yoni* (female genitalia). During prayers *ghee* is usually poured over the tip, then flowers are scattered over and sandalwood paste dabbed on. As Swamiji stood over me with this object nestled in the palm of his hand, he said, 'This is to put in your *puja* place. Shiva's *lingam* is being held in place by Shakti's *yoni*. This is the mystery of the universe. When Shakti holds Shiva the world dissolves. There is oneness. There is stillness. There is only one body. Then there is nobody.' He winked, gave me the *lingam* and then walked away. I watched him disappear, an orange flame disappearing into green. I held the smooth, shiny black *lingam* in my hand and felt so much love for Swamiji. He was the most extraordinary person — the Adonis I had been searching for.

A few days later Swamiji bestowed on me the *Sanskrit* name Archana, which means adoration or worship. He was never to call me by my old name, Mary, again. He explained that my spiritual path was to be one of adoration of the Divine and I believed him, even though the object of my adoration at this time was mostly Swamiji himself.

One full moon I experienced a love that seemed to cross boundaries of personal love. Each full moon it had become a regular ritual for the girls to dance in the Circle: a cleared area of ground near the two flagpoles from which a path ran directly to the veranda door. (The main path up to the ashram went behind the flagpoles and ran parallel to this other path from this Circle.) Around the Circle were garden beds full of flowers and shrubs.

For the first few months I refused to join in these events and would watch from a distance. When Mariana was here, she and Saraswati would dance freely and with abandon to music played on one of Swamiji's many tape-recorders. After Mariana ran away, Saraswati danced alone. A favourite was Paul Horne's 'Flute in the Taj Mahal'. At first Swamiji tried to goad me into joining them but when I declined he said, 'Wait a few months. I'll have you unblocked by then'.

In November, Saraswati went to Delhi for a few

The Serpent Rising

days to arrange a visa extension. The full moon came during this time and Swamiji said, 'Tonight you will dance for me'. I felt nervous but went and bathed, put on a new white robe, sprinkled sandalwood perfume on my wrists and around my neck and placed jasmine flowers in my hair. I then walked hesitantly into the Circle, glad that Saraswati was not there. Swamiji was sitting up on the roof of the main building outside the Meditation Room with a tape recorder.

When the music began playing I moved slowly at first, with my back to Swamiji. Then I felt something unlock inside of me and found myself moving freely, almost uncontrollably as if I was being taken over. It was enthralling. I whirled and twirled and was quite amazed by the graceful and intricate movements my hands and fingers were making. My whole body moved rhythmically. For hours it seemed I danced and moved while Swamiji changed the tapes when they had finished. Sometimes I noticed him sitting there watching me. At other times he was lying on his back on the *charpoi* he left outside during the summer months. Most of the time I forgot he was there.

Later that night when we were lying together on the roof, for the first time I didn't feel as if Swamiji was raising my energy. This time our *'kundalini* raising' was not quick but prolonged as we rocked gently like waves in a quiet harbour. I felt myself moving in and out of his body and began to feel my forehead blazing with light. At times it was if my whole body was full of light. When I gazed up at the moons and the stars in the dark mantle above the whole universe seemed to be dancing in light and we were a part of and not separated from this creation. On this night I truly felt as if I was Radha, the most beloved of the *gopis*, with whom Krishna sported in the *lila* of love.

Life would have been idyllic for me if Swamiji and I had just played at being Radha and Krishna. During these first five months, the sexual aspect of our relationship did not disturb me. But as well as being my beloved, my Krishna (the stealer of the hearts of the *gopis*), Swamiji was also the teacher, Rudra as he called it — the destructive aspect of Shiva. This was the facet of Swamiji's personality that he seemed to be able to turn on and off at will. It scared me and I found it very difficult to accept and understand.

At these times dreadful expressions crossed his face. His eyes would widen and bulge outwards and the whites would blaze with red. His voice would also change and reach a high pitch, even a screech. I had never before witnessed anything like it. It was as if he had turned into a madman, if not a demon. It was terrifying to me, especially in the beginning.

Sometimes he would grab a long stick that was kept for chasing away monkeys or wild animals and he would beat one of the boys across the legs, on their buttocks or even across their backs. He would scream at them and call them *kudaboxes*. He often told them they were sleeping and he had to beat them to wake them up.

The kitchen was the place where Swamiji most often became Rudra. He was like a Zen master where food preparation was concerned. Everything had to be done with total attention and rhythm. If he caught anyone being clumsy or inattentive, then the culprit would be sent out with a slap on the face, a tug on the ear and a tirade of abusive words to accompany them. It was in or near the kitchen that suddenly aspirants, especially the boys, would be overcome with a craving for food. But Swamiji insisted that this craving was not hunger but greed. He claimed that for centuries yogis in the upper reaches of the Himalayas have lived for months, even years, on *prana* alone. Hence it was just conditioning and habit that produced the sensation of hunger in the stomach. We were taught that we simply did not need to eat as much as we thought we did. Hunger (along with other natural desires) was an enemy we had to fight and conquer.

The boys were obviously confused about Swamiji's distinction between hunger and greed and this reflected in their actions around the kitchen. They would drop buckets of water, allow the buffalo milk to boil over or let the fire go out. I was astonished to see how their faces changed when they worked near the kitchen and I tried to ignore the slightly crazed looks that came over them. Their eyes would widen and dart everywhere. Also they would begin to move here and there without finishing one task at a time. When they became like this, Swamiji would send them away usually to the back of the Kriya Room or even to the toilets where he said they belonged. Occasionally he would do this to one of us girls but we were sneakier and also got away with more things generally around Swamiji. We became skilled at sneaking food into our mouths behind Swamiji's back without becoming flustered or confused.

Sometimes I heard the boys arguing in the Kriya Room over whose turn it was to go to the post office to fetch the mail or to buy provisions from the market place. They used these journeys as an excuse to buy sweets and other food, which they would then try and sneak back into the ashram. Swamiji would regularly inspect their bags and backpacks and would even look carefully though the shelves in the Kriya Room. Often he found foods they had hidden and would chuck them down one of the toilets. He would scream out that they were pigs. Sometimes he would pull their hair or shake them. Once he dragged Angus into one of the water tanks, pushed his head under the water and held it down for a few seconds.

At first I was appalled by such acts and would rush to intervene. This would infuriate Swamiji and even the boys didn't appreciate it. They seldom protested against these acts of violence and seemed to enjoy them. They believed they were benefiting spiritually from Swamiji's wrath — the divine wrath of Rudra. It was sickening to hear them apologising or pleading forgiveness. Occasionally I noticed Saraswati or one of the others watching and smirking while Swamiji gave one of his 'lessons' (as he called them). The experience of observing fellow disciples being woken up seemed to have the effect of raising their own spirits.

For my part, however, at least in the early days, all this made me want to run away. At least once a week I would rush back to the Shakti Kutir and pack my possessions. I would feel frantic and become convinced that Swamiji was a madman and dangerous. He always sensed when I was packing my things and he would appear with a smile. His Rudra had been switched off and he would revert to being my beloved Lord Krishna. My fear would vanish. And then I would feel foolish and realise he was in complete control after all. He just assumed Rudra to teach us lessons. The problem was in me alone — I was lacking in faith and needed to surrender more to him.

It was many months before he even raised his voice at me. He used to say, 'Little mouse would freak out if I give her a lesson. She will run away and we will never see her again'. He was probably right.

Towards the end of the rainy season Angus ran away during the night. Nobody saw him leave and it wasn't until morning that we realised he had gone. He had either scaled one of the high gates or perhaps he had found a small gap in the barbed wire fence. When Swamiji learnt that he had disappeared he went into his room and stayed there all morning.

At midday he called for me. I was shocked at the sight of him. He was lying in bed with a hand-knitted woollen hat on and was hugging several blankets around himself, even though it was not cold. I sat on the floor below him and noticed he had been crying as his eyes were red and swollen and his face was pale and drawn.

When I asked him why he was so sad, he replied in a soft, wretched voice that was almost a whisper, 'This "teacher of mine", this "teaching nature" makes me sad because I have to hurt my beloved disciples. I don't want to hurt them but I am just trying to wake them up out of their sleeping consciousness. I don't want to do this but it is my karmic duty. Sometimes I just want to leave this body. I am so tired of this life. My nature is so sensitive, so transparent all my disciples' lower natures reflect on it. I am like blotting paper. When I teach, at the same time I cry inside. I want to go back home and rest in my real nature. But this is my *karma*. I have to wake up those I love the most in the world. For we have all been together before, many, many times on the seesaw of *samsara*. You have all been with me before in India. You have been yogis and you have all abused your power.'

I had no idea what to say to him. A deep ache grew in my chest as if my heart was being squeezed tightly. He seemed like a fragile little child, a child of God and surely it was my duty to stay here forever to take care of him.

For the rest of the day I was more convinced than ever that Swamiji was one of the most enlightened beings on the planet. I realised also that that made me pretty special — one of the few chosen ones on this planet to be near this person. Perhaps, besides Swamiji, we were the oldest souls in the world and therefore the closest to 'enlightenment'! Surely there was no one in the world functioning at Swamiji's level. He himself said that all the god-men and proclaimed *avatars* rising to glory in India and flying overseas were just conmen or magicians operating at a very low level to lure the masses. Some were saintly beings but they lacked the awareness to accompany it.

But there were times when Swamiji was neither Rudra nor Krishna. He was just a little boy-yogi. Most days about mid-morning (if things were flowing peacefully) there was supposed to be an hour hatha yoga class on the roof of the Kriya Room but these were more a chance for Swamiji to show off than instruct us in new or improved ways of performing these yoga positions. He was able to do most difficult *asanas* with ease and one of his favourites was to lift both his legs behind his shoulders and wrap them around his neck. I used to wonder what was the point of these contortions but never had the courage to ask. When Swamiji was locked into one of these positions he would call out, 'Look, look at me,' like a child showing off to some friends. I'd feel irritated by him at these times and would move my mat further away and do my own routine: shoulder stands, headstands or simple posterior stretches or spinal twists.

When Swamiji did these exercises he would wear a skimpy orange loincloth and so loose around the legs that tufts of black pubic hair would stick out the sides. Sometimes even his testicles would squish out like folds of chicken skin. He had the habit of tugging at a clump of pubic hair twisting it several times between his thumb and forefinger and then he would smell his fingers and say: 'Yogi smell. My body has a pure smell. No worldly vibrations. I like to check the smell of my body to see if it needs any cleaning'.

Apart from his face and his genitals, his body was like that of a young pubescent boy. He was in superb physical condition with no excess fat and his skin was soft as a baby's like satin to touch. Saraswati told me that Swamiji was over forty years old but no one knew his exact age, not even Swamiji, or so he said. He could not remember the year in which he was born for as a young boy he had run away from his home in a small village near Ahmedabad and had no contact with his family again. Though reluctant to talk about this past he once commented that his entire extended family had slept in one small room sharing two cots. He remembered being disturbed at night by strange noises and movements coming from his parents and vowed he would never become a householder and indulge in such worldly activities.

One day he decided to run away and become

a renunciate in the Shankaracharya tradition. He walked barefoot to Hardwar nestled in the foothills of the Himalayas and there at one of the ashrams learnt basic yoga *asanas*, *kriyas* and *pranayama*. When he had mastered all they could teach him, he walked all the way up the Himalayas to the source of the Ganges, Gangotri. He claimed that he spent years there in a cave in the snow and wore only a loincloth. He further claimed that he had very few possessions and only a single pot for carrying, cooking and eating food. Relying on passing pilgrims for donations of food, he had no food on some days so he would either rummage for tree roots or seeds or simply fast. Most of his time was spent in deep meditation.

Swamiji told people that during these years of austerity he learnt to control the elements and communicate with great souls past and present on this planet, making contact with all the great *avatars* including Gautama the Buddha and Jesus the Christ. It was only time before stories of his greatness filtered down the mountain and Indian disciples sought him out and bestowed on him the mantle of guru. Ten years ago one of these disciples purchased five acres of land, and arranged for buildings to be constructed there and donated it all to Swamiji: the beginning of his International Yogant Academy. Swamiji said he reluctantly left the source of Ganga to come down to begin what he called 'his teaching phase'.

Three years ago he had his first contact with a Westerner — an American lady named Tapasya — and from that time he had allowed select Westerners to come here and stay. Tapasya had stayed for only one year. Swamiji told me the story of how she seduced him one night and from this new experience he discovered a powerful way of awakening the *kundalini* of his female disciples. However Tapasya had run away on discovering he was sharing his energy with Saraswati (who had began living at the ashram about eleven months after Tapasya had first come here).

I heard these stories of Swamiji's — of his distant and recent past — and believed them. There was no reason to doubt the details of his physical journey and more and more I began to believe that he did have the spiritual powers that he and his disciples claimed he had.

Months passed and it seemed that I had been living at this isolated jungle ashram for years even decades. In this isolated introspective community the only divisions of time I now took notice of were night, day, and mealtimes. What day it was, or even what month it was, ceased to have any importance. We never listened to the radio or read newspapers and so had no idea about what was going on in the world at large or even India itself.

However, because of Swamiji's teachings we became acutely aware of the weather and the changing seasons. He taught us that the images of the gods and goddesses we worshipped, our ideas of the divine, were reflected in nature or projected onto it. Thus the rain was tears, the sorrow of separation. The mountains were the abode of some of the gods and goddesses especially of Shiva who high on a Himalayan peak dallied with his consort Parvati or sat in the stillness of his real nature in deep meditation. Some of the pictures in the ashram depicted Shiva's head as a peak of the Himalayan with his long, curling locks as the neighbouring hills and that mighty river Ganga flowing downwards through these locks like a hissing serpent. In other pictures Shiva is sitting quietly in the hills with serpents, snakes wrapped around him and slithering over him. The serpent in Hinduism is *maya* — the mind's veil of illusion projected onto the world.

These legends are still very much a part of everyday Indian life. I became so absorbed in them that they became part of my life as well. God was not a benevolent old father in the heavens isolated from me as he had been in the Christian religion of my childhood. God was now close to me. Parabrahma of the Hindu religion is believed to be manifest throughout the universes, reflected in all things but also the unmanifest, the unknowable, that from where all things came.

During *satsang* I learnt that running through the diverse beliefs and practices of Hinduism is the belief in one God that manifests in multifarious ways in the cycles of moons, stars and galaxies, the growth and death of living things. The profusions of gods and goddesses represent different aspects of this manifestation. Thus Kali and Durga are depicted as fierce to symbolise the destructive side of life — the destroying of evil. Saraswati is the goddess of wisdom and Krishna the god of divine love. Despite the profusion of gods and goddesses in Hinduism, it is not a polytheistic religion as there is agreement amongst Hindus that there is one God — 'ek Bhagwan'.

Hinduism delighted and enthralled me. I became immersed in it, learn its ways and rituals, learnt countless *Vedic* prayers by heart as well as long sections of the holy books including the *Bhagavad-Gita* and the *Ramayana*. Swamiji, this yogi who I was beginning to accept as my guru and whom Saraswati and the others claimed was God-incarnate, guided us into the poetry and mystery of Hinduism and *Vedanta* philosophy.

But Swamiji refused to acknowledge who or what he was. He would say there are many levels of spiritual awakening and at the final stage there would be no need to live in a physical body on this planet. One would be reabsorbed and the body would disintegrate, perhaps burst into fire and return to the elements from which it came.

He would say: 'What does it matter who I am, what I am? You have no concept of my consciousness. The intellect cannot comprehend such notions. The only thing you need is faith. You need to surrender to me. The guru's task is to lead you from darkness to light. My job is to take you way from the darkness of your lower natures and lead you to your real nature, which is inside of you. Your real nature is your true guru. When you are in touch with your own guru inside of you, you won't need me. When my work is done I will leave this body. One day you will finally understand. People talk about being in touch with God. All these gurus around India. That is just nonsense. God is like the central powerhouse. If you touched it you'd explode from the high voltage. God's power can only be transformed and filtered down onto this planet. Most of these gurus have only "realised" themselves, but that is only the beginning of the road. People get stuck there. They think they have arrived home. Then all the sheep start coming. All the tired, world-weary Westerners start flocking to them and support the gurus' dreams of being awakened. You disciples of mine are very old souls. That is why you have come to me. We have been together in many other lives. But your problem is that you have become attached to me. That is not Love.'

So many Westerners came. Usually they wanted to stay. Most were turned away. Day after day between 2p.m. and 5 p.m., the world-weary and the curious trudged up the winding path, past the two orange flags waving on top of the high bending poles, past our sacred Circle and into our magical garden — a place ablaze with flowers, full of the smell of eucalyptus leaves and jasmine flowers and where doves called to each other.

There were Indian visitors too, but they came only for *darshan* and *satsang*. They were content to live in the world outside, in family life — the stage of life called *grihastha* (the householder).

Many of the Westerners who came thought this could be a place to stay and rest and perhaps to learn to cope with their wretched lives. Some did stay a few days, a few weeks, sometimes even a month or two, but seldom longer. For behind the façade of beauty and tranquillity was Swamiji's teaching nature. He was easily angered and his so-called 'lessons' often seemed irrational and absurd. Our beliefs seesawed. Most of the time he appeared to be an enlightened *tantric* master operating beyond our feeble human conceptions of good and evil or right and wrong. This enabled us to rationalise that through his lessons he deliberately created chaos so that our petty egotistical minds would be stilled, exhausted, and at last transcended. At other times and in another mood, we believed he was a madman, out of control — a devil playing games with gullible disciples.

For some of us, if we did not believe in Swamiji

and maintain our faith, then the whole structure of our dreams of becoming more spiritual would crumble around us. To doubt him we discovered led not only to confusion but distress.

We had two alternatives — to leave or to stay. To leave would mean returning to the lives we were tired of, dissatisfied with. To stay would mean that, in spite of the harshness of Swamiji's teachings, we would taste things we had never tasted before and probably would be unlikely to taste anywhere else: the taste of the sublime; *kundalini* fire rising up our spinal columns; our third eye centres opening into light and our hearts melting into ecstasy.

Chapter 7

Monkey Mind

Despite the growing sense of timelessness that life at the ashram induced, certain problems related to time began to occupy my mind. There was always the problem of money, for example. By November, after five months here, I had only 1000 rupees left. However, there was still the money in New Zealand that the insurance company had sent to my mother. I estimated that this money could last me a few more years in India as well as provide an airfare home in an emergency. I wrote to my mother asking her to send me over a few hundred dollars in the form of a bank draft to one of the major Indian banks in New Delhi. Within weeks a message was received from the bank to say they were holding the draft for me. Since there was no telephone at the ashram, I went down to Swargashram Office and asked the postmaster to telephone the bank to say I would be coming in a few days to collect my money.

But when I told Swamiji I needed to go down to Delhi, he shook his head and, when he spoke, his voice was uncharacteristically shrill, as if my words had hurt him in some way. 'Money's not important here. You can stay here forever if you like. This is your real home. Leave the money in Delhi for a while. Everyone comes here and wants to leave straight away. They use any excuse and go running back into the world again to get covered in dreams. They forget their guru who tried so hard to wake them up. Such is the pull of *samsara*. Do you want to end up like Mariana? At the bottom of the ocean.'

I was sitting on the floor and he was standing next to me, his robe brushing against my face. Nearby, the coals on the portable *barossi* fire were gleaming, orange on black and the sweet smell of freshly picked eucalyptus leaves, burning slowly, drifted towards me. Winter was almost here. Nobody slept on the roof any more.

As Swamiji spoke to me, his toes (peeking out from his orange robe) rubbed and stroked my feet. I remembered how Sai Baba had done the same thing. His voice dropped and became soft and silky, 'Little mouse is trying to run away already? Haven't you learnt your lesson yet? Look at the big changes happening inside of you. You are becoming very sensitive. Lots of *kundalini* energy being awakened. From this: (he rubbed his two fingers together) one and one make one'.

At these words, spoken so seductively, my plans melted away. I just sat there with nothing to say. As I sat there I realized there was a part of my mind that would always agree with him, which would see that what he said was in some way right for me. When he spoke like this, the questioning, analytical processes of my mind usually switched off. Those processes that in the past had been so overused that at times they had burnt out.

Though I didn't tell Swamiji, there was a second

reason why I had also felt like leaving. Over the last few months I had noticed myself changing dramatically. For example, when I carried out even the simplest of tasks, such as sweeping the veranda, I was often aware of not only my whole body moving rhythmically, but also, the sensation of my hand gripping the straw broom and even how my eyes focused on the floor I was cleaning. There was no rushing to complete the job. There was no daydreaming about other things. Just sweeping the floor attentively. When there was such attention, my mind became peaceful and joyous. It seemed I was becoming less the robot I used to be — a machine performing certain actions whilst my mind was far away, here and there, running into the future or dwelling on the past.

Things were slowing down at last and I was beginning to realize there was the profoundest joy to be had in the experiencing of the smallest things. Listening to the doves calling and the Ganga roaring, smelling the jasmine flowers in the garden and the various herbs growing wild in the jungle, watching the stars blaze in the skies at night and the sun rising and sinking all became intense experiences for me. I also noticed my face was looking younger, my eyes softer and clearer. Even Swamiji pointed this out to me. 'You see, Archana. Much change. *Kundalini* purifying. Cleaning out your body and your mind. Now, sometimes, you look sixteen years again. This happens to people when they come here. Though, when you freak out and lose faith in me, want to run away, then you look fifty years old — old and tired. Just look at your eyes — very clear now.'

Although awed by this transformation, I sometimes questioned it. How permanent was this change? Would I lose it all, away from this ashram? I needed to know whether I could live out there, anywhere, and feel the same way as I did here. If not, then what was the point of being here at all?

From the time I learnt my draft had arrived in Delhi, the germ of restlessness began to unsettle me. Swamiji sensed it. 'It's just your monkey mind. The trouble with you Westerners is that you have no self-control. Be detached. Watch this mind of yours. The mind is very cunning and very dangerous.'

However, I didn't know how to watch my mind, my thoughts. Instead I tried to fight against the restlessness, to push it aside. Finally it got so bad that in meditation class and *satsang* I could barely sit still for longer than five or ten minutes. I would begin to fidget and usually made excuses to leave the class. I'd go around the back of the Kriya Room and wash my clothes or try to keep busy in other ways. Finally one morning I made up my mind to leave, at least temporarily, not only to collect my money but also to test myself outside. Swamiji reluctantly gave me permission.

As I was leaving, I knelt down to touch and kiss Swamiji's feet. He put his hand gently on my head. 'Just remember this is your home, the garden of your heart. It's just your mind taking you outside. There's no need to go anywhere. Have a taste out there and come back soon.'

A loud squawking made me turn around. A black crow was sitting on the bench outside Saraswati's room. I looked up at Swamiji and noticed he was looking across at the bird. 'This is a very bad omen. You should not go at this time. That bird is the messenger of the devil.'

I ignored him, stood up and waited for him to put

the red *tilak* mark on my forehead. As I walked down the path, I looked back and saw Swamiji standing outside the veranda door, watching me. An orange flame against the jungle green. I waved and then began to run down the spiral path towards the gate. The crow flew overhead, squawking wildly. Tears streaked my face.

The boats were running again. During the heavy rains of the rainy season, they seldom cross the swollen Ganga. In the past years a few boats had tipped over in mid-stream flinging hundreds of pilgrims into cold, raging waters. As we moved away from the bathing ghats of Swargashram, I looked across to the jungle-clad mountains behind. The few buildings on the ridge could not be seen; the deodar firs and other trees towered around them, like an almighty shield. The only sign of the ashram was the orange flags waving on the two poles that crossed each other about midway. The flagpoles reminded me of Swamiji rubbing his forefingers together, symbolizing the union of two bodies. These past months were truly the most extraordinary of my life.

I looked down into the blue-green water and let my hand hang loosely over the side of the boat. This icy cold water had first trickled out from a cave called Gomukh in the snout of a glacier 100 kilometres away and was now leaping downwards on its long journey a further 2000 kilometres to an outlet in the Bay of Bengal, near Calcutta. Swamiji had once remarked that the mind was like the flow of water, still and clear near the source, muddy and dirty at the mouth in the ocean. He had likened the endless cycle of water (that begins from the river's mountain source and wanders downward to the sea, then moving upwards through the clouds to fall as rain in the mountains again) to the mind that moves in restless cycles looking for satisfaction in the outside world. As I sat there, I prayed that this journey would satisfy my restlessness, so I could come back here to the lap of the gods.

When we reached the other side, near the Shivananda Ashram, I clambered out of the boat and climbed into a scooter rickshaw. I glanced across the river for one last time and looked up at the tiny orange flags waving. I thought of Swamiji, my adorable boy-yogi and my heart lurched. 'I hope you know what you're doing. Haven't you found everything you ever wanted in your life up there on the hill,' I said silently to myself. I turned away and brushed the tears off my face with the palm of my hand.

Ten minutes later, we passed through Rishikesh. I had to pull the end piece of my white sari across most of my face to protect it from the dust that billowed up whenever we hit a hole in the road or a rock. The driver careered from one side of the road to another to avoid groups of pilgrims and *sadhus*. Some of the *sadhus* were naked and covered with yellow vermilion smears, their long matted hair caked with dried mud, and they carried in one hand the trident of Shiva. Small boys rode adult-sized bicycles, leaping up after each rise of the pedal so that their little bodies could slide up over the cross bar and their other foot could reach down to the opposite pedal. At first I was fascinated by these sights — this kaleidoscope of constantly changing colours and patterns — but after a while a dizziness came over me. By the time we reached Hardwar, twenty-four kilometres from Rishikesh, I felt like turning back.

Everything was moving too fast for me and I felt I was caught in a whirlpool. People seemed to have haunted looks on their faces and appeared out of control as they shuffled here and there, eyes darting, voices chattering feverishly. It occurred to me that maybe I had begun to 'wake up', to see things from a clearer level, whereas before I had been gross and insensitive from being so immersed in the world. Perhaps Swamiji was right when he said it was hell outside and most people were sleepwalkers: in a state of sleep, covered with dreams. In contrast I felt like an alien, a superior being, who had landed on some weird planet.

To fill in time before the train left, I wandered around the bazaar and on passing an open stall displaying brightly coloured milk sweets I felt my eyes widen. There was an odd sensation in my eyeballs — a swelling and bulging sensation as if they wanted to suck up and grasp all of the glistening, sugary sweet mounds before me. For a moment I had an impulse to jump up onto the stand on all fours and stuff everything into my mouth in a frenzy. I looked up at the vendor, squatting behind his tiers of sweet meats. He was grinning at me, 'English memsahib want sweeties? Very good sweets. Pure buffalo milk.'

I glanced over the display and chose some large *gulab-jamuns*, balls of flour, yoghurt, almonds and sugar. Walking back to the station, I shovelled them into my mouth, barely tasting them. I felt like crying. What on earth was happening to me? I felt completely out of control. Was I being completely overwhelmed by greed? Perhaps I was just 'picking up' the coarser vibrations of those around me. I felt fragile, almost transparent. It was as if all my nerves were raw and exposed

I sat up all night in the train. Thoughts spun around in my mind continuously and I became more and more tense. Everything around me — the noises, the movements, the smells (and perhaps even more subtle vibrations) — seemed to be impinging upon me and I had no idea how to distance myself from it all. The compartment was crowded. A group of men, squatting on the floor in one corner, chatted and laughed all night, the smoke from their *beedi* cigarettes drifting over to me. But neither these men nor any others hassled me on this train journey for I was wearing the clothes of a Hindu *sadhu*: a white cotton robe, sandalwood *mala* beads around my neck and a flame-shaped *tilak* on my forehead.

Whenever I tried to picture the ashram and Swamiji, doubts crossed my mind like dense, grey clouds crossed my mind. Why hadn't Swamiji warned me that coming outside, coming down from the Himalayan Hill, would be like this? What was the point of becoming sensitive and pure if one couldn't cope outside? Why hadn't he given me some method, a technique, to protect myself from the pressures of the ordinary world, a world in which for some obscure reason I still wanted to be able to live and to feel spiritual at the same time.

By the time the train pulled into New Delhi the next morning I was in a state of panic. I had already failed the test I had set myself. I booked into a cheap hotel at the edge of Paharganj, one street away from where I had first stayed six months ago. Paharganj acts as a sort of buffer zone between the cities of Old Delhi and New Delhi. Like Old Delhi, it has narrow lanes and is congested and noisy.

Towards mid-morning I went to the bank but to my utter disbelief the draft was not there. More than three hours were spent working my way down long queues and trudging up and down flights of stairs. Each clerk I spoke to either redirected me to another room, on another floor, or motioned me to sit down, whereupon I would wait for up to half an hour while they took breaks, made *chai* over kerosene stoves or ate snacks. Finally I became so exasperated I shouted at one of the clerks to get the manager, immediately. He soon appeared, smiling and relaxed and took me into his office. When he rang branches of the bank in other Indian cities he discovered that the draft had been sent to Calcutta on the instructions of the Swargashram postmaster. I couldn't believe it.

The bank manager advised me to go personally to Calcutta as he explained that it could take weeks for the draft to be redirected back to Delhi and then it could get lost on the way. I had finally come up against the renowned Indian bureaucracy, the maze of red tape that is said to be a legacy of the British. It was now mid-afternoon and by this time I was in such a confused state, I didn't even bother asking why the draft would take so long to be redirected.

As I was about to leave he stood up, readjusted the white *khadi lungi* wrapped around his pouching waist, and grinned broadly. His white, even teeth, sandwiched between pink gums and browny-pink, thick lips, glistened. 'Money is not everything. There is more to life than money. When you are in touch with your own Divinity, everything you need will come to you effortlessly. You English people struggle too much. Our country is very old and has many secrets for you.'

I groaned loudly and strode out glaring at everyone. These Indians infuriated me with their grins, their borrowed words of wisdom, their patience.

Dazed, I made my way back to the hotel room and lay on the sagging *charpoi* for the rest of the afternoon. The noises of Paharganj had eased a little as many shops and stalls had closed while their owners took a siesta. Thoughts whirred around in my mind. The idea of travelling to Calcutta and back, a journey of over forty hours by train, was daunting. At times I wondered whether I should escape from this city that seemed to be closing in upon me, escape and return to the Himalayas, those magnificent mountains of stillness. But then that would be cowardly of me and would mean I had completely failed outside.

In the ashram, I had begun to feel detached and had found it relatively easy to meditate, to enter into spaces of peace and joy. But now, even though completely controlled by my mind, the last thing I felt like doing was to meditate as a way to concentrate my thoughts and relax my body. Instead I just lay there with this frantic mental activity going on inside my head. Disappointed, I realized that the remarkable changes I had experienced in the ashram were transitory — the world was a wretched place after all and I felt wretched in it.

At about five o'clock, the bazaar suddenly burst into life again. I felt hungry and decided to go outside for something to eat. As I walked along the narrow street, two Australians came up and began talking to me. They had met travelling overland in a bus from England and in a few weeks would be travelling home, the girl, Deborah, by aeroplane, and the man, Joe, by hitchhiking through South East

Asia. We decided to eat together and managed to find a relatively clean restaurant a few streets away. As we sat there eating a simple meal of *chapattis*, curd and lentils, Joe looked at me intently with his soft green-blue eyes. I sensed a gentleness about him as well as an earthy ruggedness and this appealed to me.

Joe's long, black straggly hair and bushy beard reminded me of the New Zealand poet, James K. Baxter, with whom I had become friendly at a university congress some years back. James and I sometimes slipped away from the intellectual debates and went for long walks along the rocky shores. We had competitions to see who could stand on their head the longest, and, with me being an atheist and James a devout Catholic, we would have heated arguments as to the existence of God. On one occasion James looked into my eyes (similar to the way that Joe was looking at me) and said, 'One day you will be a believer. I can see it in those big brown eyes of yours. The soul is reflected in the eyes. You are deeply religious but you don't know it.' At the time I scoffed at such an idea. I would never have believed then that three years later I would sacrifice everything I had worked for, to fly away to India on a spiritual search.

Then Joe said, 'Why don't you come with us to Rajgiri, in Bihar, for a ten-day Vipassana camp? It's real cheap and a nice place to hang out. Better than getting spun out in this crazy city.'

I was relieved to hear that someone else was being bothered by city life. The idea of such a meditation course interested me as I had already heard of these courses in Buddhist meditation from some devotees of Sai Baba back in Bangalore. What made the idea even more attractive was that I realized that I could stop off at Rajgiri on my way back from Calcutta. Deborah was eager for me to go too. I managed a sort of a smile and agreed. Joe went on to talk about the meditation course he had done the previous year as well as other things he had experienced in India before going across to Europe and England. Finally he looked at me and said, 'Gee, you're a peaceful chick. What have you been doing in India?'

When I explained that I had been practising yoga in Rishikesh he replied, 'Oh, yoga's all right, up to a point. A bit suppressive though. This Buddhist stuff suits me. No surrender to a guru or anything. Something you can take back outside and use. Nice and simple. No rituals or prayers or any of that devotional stuff, which is really not suited to us Westerners. Unless we want to spend our lives shut away from the world'.

His words unsettled me, especially his phrase, 'take back outside and use'. I realized that what I had learnt with Swamiji was not helping me outside at all. Maybe this Buddhist meditation had a key for me? Perhaps yoga is an escape. It works only if you hide yourself away from the world. But I didn't want to talk about Swamiji. Instead I related some of my experiences with Sai Baba. Joe roared with laughter, 'Oh, the Baba Bugger.' Deborah looked on blankly while Joe winked at me knowingly. I felt relieved to have met them, especially as I would have some travelling companions the following day.

I went to bed that night feeling exhausted. Lying there, I stared up at the single light bulb, splattered with moths and their droppings, as it swung slowly from the dirty ceiling. My body was trembling involuntarily and there was an enormous pressure building up in my head. Even now, through the closed shutters of the window, I could hear the city roaring around me like a wild animal in a cage. Down below, vendors were still yelling out and the occasional radio blared out Western-style pop music sung in Hindi. I tried not to think of Swamiji as I lay there longing for sleep to come. I feared that memories of Swamiji and the love that I had for him would make me want to run back there, to escape from this hell.

The following day in the train Joe sat opposite me and kept eyeing me up and down, shaking his head slowly repeating, 'Oh, you're a cool chick'. His attention made me uncomfortable. I kept thinking of Swamiji. In my mind I pictured myself sailing farther and farther away from him on a vast, wild ocean whilst he stood back on the shore with his hands outstretched. At one stage Joe began reading out the rules from the Vipassana code of conduct. When he reached 'no sexual misconduct', he squinted at me and pursed his lips seductively. I felt myself tensing even though at the same time I felt flattered and my cheeks burned. Finally I said, 'Look, I'm already involved with someone, an amazing person. So I'm not available.'

Deborah nudged me, 'Just ignore him, Archana. He was carrying on like that to any decent-looking female we met on the way overland. It's just the Australian male's insecurity. They talk like that to boost their fragile egos.'

Joe wasn't offended. 'Come on. Our egos are the strongest in the world. Otherwise we wouldn't have survived in that Australian wasteland. It's just that you chicks don't know a good thing when you see it.' He pulled a comb and a mirror out of his bag and began to comb his head and even his moustache the way Swamiji used to. 'Oh, what a beautiful hunk,' Joe remarked nonchalantly as he gazed at himself. At this, Deborah leant over and kicked him in the shins and we all laughed loudly. The Indians in the overcrowded compartment watched our antics with astonishment. Sometimes I looked across at Joe and wondered whether I would ever be able to have sex with another man after Swamiji.

I still wasn't comfortable with Deborah and Joe. In some way I felt inferior, I wasn't quite one of them. They were normal. But in another way I felt superior because of what I had tasted and become with Swamiji was truly unique. As I leant back and closed my eyes, I noticed that the soft satin glow I used to feel in my face was gone. It now felt hard and tight like the shell of an old insect. Perhaps I was becoming coarser, worldlier.

Towards evening Joe and Deborah got out at Patna. I planned to meet up with them again in two days at Rajgiri, a short distance from Patna.

The following day I reached that great, sprawling city of Calcutta, with its air choked with smog, its sidewalks home to millions of poor, its Howrah Bridge crowded with thin, sweating ragged men pulling rickshaws behind them. These rickshaws often carried overweight Indians (sometimes even families) as well as mounds of their suitcases and luggage.

When I arrived at the bank I was told that no draft had ever arrived for me. The telephone lines to Delhi were out of order and it could take hours or even days for the lines to be reconnected again. The manager advised me to return to Delhi. I didn't know whether to laugh or cry.

I left Calcutta on the next train, my nose running and my eyes stinging from the smog and the dust. My impressions of this city were that it was ugly and desperate, yet others have found it fascinating, with a rare beauty. I didn't stay long enough to find anything to draw me to her. As I watched her black and grey smoky mass fade from view, I was reminded of Rudyard Kipling's often quoted lines:

> *Chance directed, chance erected, laid and built on the silt,*
> *Palace, byre, hovel — poverty and pride — Side by side;*
> *And, above the packed and pestilential town,*
> *Death looked down.*

But soon we were into the rich, green landscape of rural Bengal. The recently harvested fields were bordered by tall palms of coconut, the fronds of which looked like large, green umbrellas (under which the workers can sometimes shelter and rest). This rural India seemed worlds away from the bustling millions of Calcutta and Delhi with their extremes of poverty and riches.

The following day we approached Bihar, one of the poorest states in India. Bihar is a religious centre mostly for Buddhists, especially Tibetan Buddhists. Rajgiri was the place where the first Buddhist council was held after Gautama the Buddha attained *nirvana* and he spent twelve years here. In Bihar the orange worn by the Hindu swamis is replaced by the maroon of Buddhist monks. The maroon robes are a deep rich blood colour; their wearers pursue the path of release from pain and suffering, life and death. In contrast, the orange robes symbolize the sun, 'the realization of the Self': the goal of the Hindu.

The train, after numerous delays, reached Patna four hours behind schedule. I caught a bus to Rajgiri and by the time I had arrived there and caught a scooter-rickshaw out to the location of the camp, the course was due to start in less than half an hour. I had just enough time to wash and register for the course when a message through a loudspeaker instructed us to assemble in the Great Hall. As I was walking towards this building I caught sight of Deborah but we had only time for a few brief words when a gong struck three times signalling the beginning of *mouna*, silence. These few words to Deborah were the last I was to speak for ten days.

In the hall divided into two sections, male and female, were about three hundred people sitting cross-legged. Most eyes were directed towards a gentle-looking Indian, Goenka, who was dressed in a white *lungi* and sat on a simple chair on a bare platform. About one third of the gathering looked to be Westerners of all ages. Some were elderly, in their seventies or eighties, but most were probably in their twenties. Up on the platform there was no altar and hence no pictures of deities or gurus to idolize or worship. There were no flowers anywhere, nor incense burning.

For half an hour Goenka read out the rules of conduct in English. (Evidently courses directed in Hindi alternated monthly with those spoken in English.) These rules included no writing, reading or talking for ten days. He then gave us a brief explanation of the technique of meditation, especially the steps we were to follow this first day. To conclude, he spent a few minutes chanting a few verses in Pali. These sounds were deep and seemed to rumble from the depths of his abdomen. This chanting was a strange sound that was altogether different from the chanting of the Hindus. It was slow, almost mournful, but moved me deeply.

I closed my eyes and began to relax. The stillness and silence was heaven compared to the hellish noise and turmoil of the last few days. There was no noise at all except for Goenka's chanting. And as I relaxed, I wondered whether silence itself was the key to what I needed. I had grown so used to the quietness in the ashram that perhaps I was not meant to be living in cities any more. Maybe I had made a big drama out of nothing.

For the next ten days from 4a.m. until 9p.m. we sat in the Great Hall and meditated continuously, except for meal breaks and short periods allocated mainly for bathing and washing clothes by hand. Hour after hour for the first few days we practised *anapana*: watching our breath, the inhalation and exhalation through the nostrils. The aim of this breath-watching was to build up intense concentration after which the actual technique of Vipassana could then be practised for the remaining seven days. The latter involved attempting to watch, with equanimity, sensations that arose in the body, sensations that are ever changing, from gross to subtle.

The rationale for this observation of changing sensations in the physical body was, in part, so that the meditator can realize more fully *ducca* (suffering). Evidently if we can simply watch both pleasant and unpleasant sensations arising and falling in the body and learn not to desire the pleasant nor avoid and react to the unpleasant, then the basic habit patterns of the mind can be changed. We can come out of the misery, the suffering, that Buddhists say is 'the human condition'.

It was not difficult for me to sit still for these long hours as I was used to sitting in a half-lotus position for hours on end. But other difficulties soon appeared — the pain of confusion. It was difficult to reconcile this simple Buddhist approach with loving and serving Swamiji: the path of worship and service. The hourly discourse each evening especially was a breeding ground for my confusion since Buddhists don't talk about surrender and love, the things of the heart. They talk about witnessing and alertness, things of the head.

Excruciating pains began to form in my head as I tried to ignore the conflicting trains of thought that charged relentlessly through my mind. Each time I attempted to watch the changing sensations in other parts of my body, within seconds I was back in my head, entangled in a web of confusion and fighting against the pain and pressure that had built up all over my forehead, temples, face and neck. At times I found myself full of fear and doubting Swamiji. I wondered whether he was in some way tuned into me, trying to control my mind, to pull me away from this simple and clear meditation. But then I would remember the love, the bliss, the sheer magic experienced at the ashram and my doubts and fear would evaporate. Sometimes the conflict and the pain in my head became so intense I broke down and cried and buried my head in my hands. Occasionally I heard the sounds of other meditators (sighs and cries, groans and yawns) rising in the hall and fading away again.

However there was something about this simple Buddhist approach that was very appealing and for short periods I experienced an extraordinary stillness that swept waves and waves of peace through me. However these times were short and infrequent because I couldn't get Swamiji out of my thoughts. I felt possessed by him. Possessed by his love or possessed by his power — an evil power?

During one of the short breaks outside the hall, I glanced out across miles and miles of patterned rice fields. Women in brightly coloured saris moved together rhythmically, as they slashed the long grasses. Naked children ran and played all around them. I thought how simple my life would be if I could just be one of them, an Indian peasant woman. Why was my life such an endless struggle? These women seemed to accept the life they are born into and which they seem powerless to change. It was mystifying to me that even those in desperate poverty, in some strange way, seemed happy and content. They laugh and smile a lot and their dark eyes sparkle. Seldom do they look despairing. Yet many of their Western counterparts who live in comparative affluence seem haunted by despair and loneliness. Perhaps it is the Hindu religion. Perhaps their beliefs give them an acceptance of their condition, an acceptance that is different from resignation. And here I was torn between two religions, with no peace of mind, no detachment.

Finally, on the tenth day, towards the end of the course, we were introduced to a short 'meta-meditation', a meditation in 'loving kindness', and as I sat there, the pain in my head easing slightly, my heart filled with warmth. I remembered my love for Swamiji and realized that I should never have tried practising Vipassana. You can't mix paths. I had to choose between love and awareness. Love had usually won in my life.

However, my mind was changed shortly

afterwards because soon after the gong had been struck to signal the end of the course and I met up with Deborah and Joe, I learnt two things. Joe had also had a difficult time. 'I kept looking over at you. You looked as though you were going through hell. Your face sometimes screwed up and several times I saw you with your head in your hands or with tears running down your face. But, you know, that really turned me on. Finally Goenka called me up. He was furious. He said I was breaking one of the rules of conduct and if I didn't stop looking at you, he'd send me away. We were meant to be looking inward, not outward. He also said I was probably affecting your meditation, thought transference or something. From then on, whenever he looked at me he seemed to be glaring at me. But that didn't stop me fantasizing. I had to do something to ease the boredom of it all. If only I could sit back and watch this lust of mine, let it all float past and disappear, but you know when I try to watch it, it just gets bigger, grows out of control.'

Deborah and I laughed. Then I told them why the course had been so difficult for me and about my tug-of-war between Buddhism and Swamiji. Joe looked surprised, 'You mean that Swami Chidanananda at the Shivananda Ashram? He's pretty harmless.'

When I explained that Joe had just assumed I had been studying there but in fact I had been at another ashram, further up the river and on the other side, a look of alarm crossed his face. 'Not that boy-yogi creep? That Balyogi Premvarni?' When I nodded, he reached over and shook my shoulders. 'Look, you're not going back there. That guy's dangerous. He takes over your mind and plays about with power. And from what I've heard, screws you as well.'

The Serpent Rising

I was stunned. Joe knew of Swamiji because he had known a girl who had stayed there for a few months. The girl had gone back to Australia and was so confused she had ended up in a psychiatric hospital. I looked out across the restful interweaving fields below us. Joe's words were like a bolt of lightning entering my brain. So that was why this Vipassana camp had been so tortuous. So that was why my life had been such hell since I left the ashram. Swamiji was tuned in to me, trying to control my brain, using his power to draw me back to him. Things started to make sense. In those few seconds I lost my faith in Swamiji. Just as my mind had changed course after the comments by Joanna (the American woman in Bangalore), the strange process had happened again. I was now on another track careering in another direction, carried along by doubt. My love had turned to hate, my faith to fear. I felt devastated, especially when I realized that all this had happened before. I had just not learnt my lesson. Somehow I had managed to be hypnotized by Swamiji.

Everything began to speed up in my head. I felt frantic. Swamiji must be possessed by some demonic energy. Perhaps he himself doesn't know what he is doing. I told Joe and Deborah to stop calling me Archana, to use my real name, Mary. Then I explained that I would have to go back to the ashram and collect my belongings. My passport was in Swamiji's safe along with other documents, birth certificate, references and such things. Joe tried to talk me out of going back but Deborah said she would come with me, as her plane for Australia did not leave for another week.

Even though an enormous sense of relief swept

through me as I began to understand the underlying reason for all my pain and confusion I knew I would not be able to relax and feel truly myself again until the rest of my possessions had been retrieved from the ashram. As I packed my things I could sense a darkness hovering about my head. It was as if Swamiji perhaps knew my change of heart, that I had woken up. With a sinking feeling, I remembered having this same feeling after escaping the clutches of Sai Baba. Would I ever learn? Why was I so gullible? What was wrong with me?

When Deborah and I were ready, we went back to say goodbye to Joe. By this time most of the meditators had disappeared, like ants scrambling down the hill towards the coffee shops and sweet stalls of the nearest bazaar. Joe walked closer to me and put his arms around me. On the verge of tears, I buried my head in his chest. He whispered, 'I'd come with you now, but all that meditation has released all this *kundalini* energy.'

As the two of us walked down the hill, he stood there watching. He called out, 'See you back in the real world, Mary. We can practise *tantra* yoga all night and day.' His words moved me. I was tempted to run back up to him. I longed to be held and sighed upon, to be wanted and to be comforted. Would I ever be able to be with men again? I realized that I was now burdened with the notion that sex with 'ordinary' men is profane and defiles one's psyche!

That night as we lay on the narrow bunks on a train heading for Hardwar, I told Deborah the story of the boy-yogi, what he did with our minds and what he did with our bodies, the *catoris* of seminal juices mixed with cream and honey and all the stains on the orange sheets. Although I felt in some way I was betraying Swamiji, that in the telling of these things I was committing some dreadful sin, I reassured myself. Why should one have to hide things? Why were Swamiji's sexual activities kept secret from the boys in the ashram? What a hypocrite!

We reached Hardwar early the next morning and took a taxi straight to the Laxman Jhula Bridge as I wanted to collect my things as quickly as possible. We climbed up the path towards the ashram. Strangely enough, the bottom gate was already open. It was as if Swamiji was expecting us. I had originally intended to try and scale the barbed wire fence and walk up unannounced because I didn't want Swamiji to be psychologically prepared for us.

When we trudged up the final snaking path of the ashram, I noticed Saraswati standing near the flagpoles. She looked ghostly as she huddled there with a large, white shawl wrapped around her body and lapping over her head. Her face was white and drawn, her eyes red and swollen. She came towards me with her arms outstretched. I stepped back. She stopped and put her hands together instead, bowing her head slightly.

'Hari Om, Archana-Ji. Swamiji's been very sick ever since you left. He knows what you've been through. You've been breaking his heart.' She began to cry.

I laughed. 'Don't call me Archana. My name's Mary. Anyway I thought I was Swamiji's heart! How can I be breaking his? I thought Swamiji was enlightened. That's what you kept telling me. How can he be, when he is so attached to us? You're not going to talk me into staying. I've just come to collect my things and get the hell out of this crazy place.' I turned to Deborah, 'You see what I mean!'

Saraswati fell on the ground and with a choking voice spluttered, 'Archana, what are you saying? This is your divine home. We are divine sisters. You've just been caught up in a dream outside. Surely you understand by now what Swamiji is doing. The sacrifices he is making for us? He's so sensitive, so transparent.'

'What a load of crap,' I replied and then strode around her and up the path. I didn't want to listen to anything else she said. I felt sick. Her words had sent a creepy shiver through me and I realized it was imperative to get out of this place as soon as possible. I went straight round to the Kriya Room and began rummaging around for anything that might belong to me. I paused a few minutes to consider whether to take my mats, buckets and *resai* with me, but decided they were too heavy to lug down the hill and across the bridge. I didn't feel like leaving anything that was mine in this wretched place and felt overwhelmed by possessiveness and pettiness.

After frantically stuffing as much as I could into some shoulder bags, I then ran back to the Shakti Kutir to collect my books, pictures, incense holders and other items. Two of the brass incense holders belonged to Swamiji, but I shoved them in as well. When I had finished, I struggled around to the main building and caught sight of Michel and Jorgen hovering near the back gate. They had sheepish grins of their faces. I glared at them. Approaching the veranda door, I heard the sounds of Deborah and Swamiji laughing and I panicked. He had conned her, used his powers to charm her. I called out, 'Swamiji, I want my things from your safe.'

The Serpent Rising

He pulled across the curtain. 'I want to talk to you alone,' he said softly. 'No, there's nothing to talk about,' I retorted. I wanted my voice to sound strong and in control, but somehow the words just whimpered out.

Swamiji laughed. 'What's got into you! Some evil spirit? What is there away from your Himalayan home? Haven't you learnt your lesson yet?'

'Give me my things now, Swamiji, or I'll go down and get the police.' My voice rose even more. I felt my cheeks reddening and I was shaking all over. Swamiji however looked in complete control and was apparently unaffected by my negativity. I loathed him for being so calm. He turned around and walked back inside and let the curtain fall so I was standing there alone and could not see inside.

A few minutes later he brought out my bag and smiled at me seductively. 'Won't you come in and take some rest. Have a cup of tea. Your friend wants to wait here a while.' I glared at him, 'Tell Deborah I'll meet her downside.' I picked up my things and bolted down the path without looking back. When I reached the downside gate, I kicked it open and collapsed on the edge of the bench outside. I was shaking all over. Deborah appeared about five minutes later looking very pleased with herself. I barked out to her, 'Quickly, I want to get away from this place. Didn't you see how Swamiji was trying to cover my mind; use his power to make me stay? I'm freaked.'

To my astonishment, she replied, 'Hang on! What's up with you? What on earth are you frightened of? This place is nothing like what you described. And Swamiji is absolutely beautiful. He couldn't hurt anyone. In fact he's an absolute doll. I think you're the one who's crazy.'

I was stunned. I did feel crazy but that didn't change my view of Swamiji. 'Look, you have no idea what he's like, what he does to your mind. It's very subtle. You've just seen one side of him. You wouldn't think like that if you'd seen him in an angry mood. He goes completely off his head. Beats the boys and the servants with long thick sticks. Once he pulled Saraswati's hair so hard he pulled a large clump out of her skull. Look, he's just conned you too. I'm going. You're a bloody traitor.'

Quickly, I walked down the path towards the Ganges feeling very freaked out. I was now convinced that Swamiji was dangerous and had used his yogic powers to control me. I was frightened that perhaps he would continue to control me. I felt like curling myself up into a tight ball and howling. After a few hundred yards Deborah caught up with me. 'You know. He asked me to stay there.'

It was as if she was trying to torment me! Angrily, I said: 'And you know what for? To get you into bed. And how can you reconcile that trip up there with all the Buddhist teachings we've just listened to?'

'There's no conflict,' she said self-assuredly. 'It's just different viewpoints. In fact I think they're saying the same thing, the Hindus and the Buddhists. It's all to do with not identifying with the mind and the body.'

Reluctant to get involved in any philosophical discussion, I didn't reply. I felt tense and terribly lonely. As we walked up the road towards the bridge, the hordes of *sadhus* sitting on the sides of the roads begging seemed to yell at me louder than usual. I snarled at some of them. One of them, naked except for a grubby loin cloth, was stretched out on a bed of six inch nails. He smiled broadly at me as I walked past. Madman, I thought. Jabbering monkeys with beady eyes watched us intently as they perched from branches towering over us. Sometimes one would swing out towards us. Then I would pick up a stick and wave it, shouting, 'Jowl, jowl, you little bastards.'

I was utterly fed up with this country, the dust, the wails and pleas of beggars, the pestering of monkeys, the slothful swamis and the lecherous yogis and I was sick to death of the colours of ochre and orange found everywhere.

Chapter 8

All The Answers

With my former name reclaimed and my valuables retrieved from the clutches of Swamiji, I left the abode of the Rishis and journeyed down to Hardwar convinced that I would never return. Surely the Devil rather than God dwelt in those regions.

Deborah and I caught the overnight train to Delhi. We hardly spoke to each other. I sat there huddled in a large grey blanket and stared out at the blackness. I didn't seem to be able to learn. How had I managed to get caught up into another religious cult? What was wrong with me?

We reached Delhi about 5.00am the next morning. Deborah went off to stay at the luxurious Chevron hotel to use up her remaining rupees, as it was illegal for her to take Indian currency out of the country. I felt she had betrayed me by taking sides with Swamiji and wondered whether she had done this out of jealousy, because of Joe's amorous attentions towards me. We parted ways without resolving the broken communication. I caught a rickshaw to Paharganj and booked into the same miserable cheap hotel I had stayed at a few weeks earlier.

It was mid-winter now, early January. Delhi froze and I was told that people were dying each day on the footpaths and in the gutters, the only homes some had ever known. Many, curled up in tattered blankets, looked as if they were sleeping but perhaps this was their final sleep. I couldn't look too closely. I was too obsessed with my own problems: my missing bank draft and trying to erase Swamiji out of my mind.

Little fires sprang up everywhere on the sides of the road, people burnt anything they could scavenge including dried cow dung and scraps of paper. There were no rubbish bins or refuse collection in Old Delhi. There was no need. Everything was recycled. For days I hung around these fires as winds crept and whooshed around corners chilling me to the bone. Every half hour or so I would buy some steaming hot milky *chai* (served in tall glasses) to warm my hands and stomach. Some days I drank about fifteen glasses. For food I ate *chapatti* bread, yoghurt and bananas as I couldn't be bothered eating anything else.

The manager of the bank again contacted their branch at Calcutta but this time he was told that they had never at any stage received a draft for me. I didn't know whom to believe. The manager was very apologetic and told me to return in four days. But four days later nothing had changed. Again, the manager told me to be patient and assured me that things sort themselves out in their own time in Mother Bharat.

I spent three weeks wandering around Delhi and kept well away from other Westerners. I did not want to get caught up in another religious trip and nor did I want to mix with the Western drug addicts that roamed the streets in surprising numbers. Finally, with only 200 rupees remaining, I decided to swallow my pride and go back to the New Zealand High Commissioner to ask for help. I expected the Commissioner to think I was slightly mad to be in a similar predicament again, still wandering around India getting caught up with gurus. Perhaps he would send me back to a psychiatric hospital in New Zealand.

But he was pleased to see me and treated me as if I was quite normal. He chatted away and even scolded me (in a friendly way) for not coming and asking for help earlier. That was their job: to help fellow New Zealanders in need. After he had obtained all the necessary details from me, he ordered a servant to bring me some tea and sandwiches. When I had finished, he reassured me, saying that he was confident the whole matter would be sorted out within a few weeks as this sort of thing often happened with bank drafts. He didn't explain what actually happened and I couldn't be bothered asking. He also said to let them know when I needed money for food and lodgings.

I now planned to leave India and return to New Zealand as soon as possible. If my money didn't arrive within a month I would ask the High Commissioner to arrange for a plane ticket home that could be repaid once I was back home.

It only took three weeks for the Commissioner to locate the missing draft. It had arrived in Calcutta two months before but had been siphoned off to a branch in a neighbouring region, presumably so the bank could accumulate some interest to pocket for themselves. The Commissioner arranged for the draft to be relocated to Delhi and this time it arrived without any further problem or delay.

I went back to the Embassy Enclave one more time as the Commissioner had invited me to lunch. As I hadn't eaten properly for weeks, I was not going to turn down this offer. The diplomatic enclave, in a tiny pocket in Delhi, was very different from other parts of Delhi, especially Paharganj and Old Delhi where I had been spending most of my time. In this enclave the roads were ridiculously wide considering the sparse traffic. Large trees lined all the roads and there were beautiful gardens and parks. The houses were luxurious mansions and Western-styled. Everything was clean and tidy and there were no beggars or poor people anywhere to be seen. There was none of the noise and chaos of the rest of Delhi.

At the Commissioner's private home, a servant answered the doorbell and showed me inside. The house was a spacious mansion and reminded me of houses back in Remuera, an affluent part of Auckland where my aunt lived. The furnishings, portraits and décor were all Western in style. After I had been ushered into the dining room, the High Commissioner introduced me to his wife and we all sat down at the large dining room table. The lunch that followed, and which two other servants brought in, was delicious and by far the most scrumptious food I had tasted since leaving New Zealand. Fresh bread with New Zealand butter and cheese, unspiced vegetable soup and quiche. There was even dessert of apple shortcake, cream and ice cream.

In spite of this feast, I could not relax or feel at ease for several reasons. I had not used a knife and fork since coming to India as I quickly learnt to eat food with my right hand only. Even sitting on a chair was uncomfortable as I had become accustomed to sitting on the ground. It was also difficult to engage in polite conversation because in the ashram meals were always eaten in silence. I tried to answer the many questions they both kept firing at me but was reluctant to give them too many details in case they decided I was crazy. Occasionally one of them would remark on what an interesting adventure I appeared to be having or what a fascinating person I was. If only they knew!

Sitting there talking to them though, it suddenly occurred to me that I had experienced India (away from the ashrams that is) in a way that was far removed from their experience. It had been so easy for me to embrace the Indian culture and way of life, indeed it was like coming back to a country I knew well, even though I had not studied much about it or shown any interest in India previously. Then I recalled how often I had felt like a stranger in New Zealand, as if I didn't quite belong there. Even though there were times I seemed to have gone through mental and physical hell these past months in India, the dreadful depression and unhappiness that had haunted me in my last years at university were no longer with me. New Zealand in my memory was a ghost land of neatness and niceness where people mask their true feelings.

As I sat there trying to answer their questions, I suddenly made the decision that I would not return to New Zealand at all. I began to plan another option. I could fly to Burma and do a short Vipassana course at the U Bha Khin Monastery. From there I could travel to Thailand, to another monastery at Chang Mai that Joe had mentioned, and after some time make my way down through South East Asia until

I reached Australia. Even though I had not practised any meditation since leaving the camp, I still remembered the peace I sometimes experienced there and resolved (now my money problems had been sorted out) to try and meditate twice a day for at least 30 minutes, preferably one hour. All these things began to dart through my mind as I simultaneously kept up a polite conversation with the Commissioner and his wife.

When the meal was over the Commissioner dispatched a black limousine to take me back to my grotty hotel. Sinking back into the leather seats I smiled as the car moved like a graceful bird, gliding silently down the wide, tree-lined streets of New Delhi. When we reached Paharganj the driver realised the car was not going to fit through the narrow congested lanes. He apologised as I clambered out. I watched the long shiny vehicle edge its way back clumsily. Grinning children ran alongside it as they pressed their little faces against the clean glass leaving snail-like trails of wetness from their tongues and noses and ghostly patterns from their breath. The driver's admonishments behind closed glass were drowned by the squeals and laughter coming from the children. Watching the sheer delight of these unrestrained children, my mind changed tracks again and I wondered whether I should just stay put in India and not go to Burma and South East Asia.

My mind was back to being monkey mind. Jumping and swinging from one branch to another and even leaping from tree to tree. Part of my problem was having no direction any more. I no longer had any desire to reach a state of 'enlightenment' that the Hindus refer to as realisation of the self and the Buddhists call *nirvana*. I wanted a certain amount of peace of mind but was frightened of completely transcending the mind altogether: of the annihilation of the thought 'I am the body, I am the body'. Neither did I have any goals for worldly accomplishments — for name, fame or fortune. Indecision was back with me again. To leave India or to stay? What on earth to do with my life? My thoughts spun around in circles as I wandered aimlessly through the bazaars of Old Delhi for the rest of the day.

The next morning when I walked outside to buy an earthenware cup of thick curd, a small taxi drove up. Angus, of all people, climbed out. I turned to rush away but he shouted, 'Archana, Archana, Don't run away. Please. Swamiji wants you to come back. Not to stay. He just wants you to leave with his blessings. Some important mail has arrived at the ashram for you. It was registered.'

I asked him what he was doing back in India so soon and how he knew where to find me. And how did he know I was still in India since I could have been back in New Zealand. He grinned. 'I got back to the ashram a few weeks ago but I'm never going to leave again. I'd rather die there than go back to the West. It is hell. Swamiji says he has been in contact with you on a subtle level ever since you left. All your pain and suffering has reflected on him. Most of the time he has just shut himself up in his room. He once told us he's going to die because his beloved Archana had forgotten him. Last night, though, he told me to go and get a taxi from Laxman Jhula. If I came down here to Paharganj I would find you. You wouldn't believe it but this was one of the first streets we drove into. Swamiji also said to tell you that there are no girls in the ashram now, no *gopis*, as Saraswati has gone back to America to renew her visa.'

    I just stood there, shaking my head. I could feel a soft smile filling my face. My heart was feeling love again. I sighed. For the last two months my heart had been closed to Swamiji, my life had been without love. Now this mysterious force was flooding back, filling up the emptiness inside of me.

    I told Angus I would come back with him but wasn't going to stay. In a daze I went up to my room and packed my things to leave them with the manager of the hotel until I returned. How extraordinary that Swamiji had such power. Perhaps it's just me, my monkey mind. Why didn't I have more faith like the others there? It's just so much easier to give in and surrender. This was all too much for me to understand.

    In the taxi on the way back up to the Himalayan Hill, I slouched back in the seat and stared dreamily out of the window for most of the way. Seven hours later as we approached Hardwar I started having doubts again. What if Swamiji was a demonic person who liked to tinker with the minds of young Westerners? But then minutes later I'd consider a different point of view — that of Swamiji being an enlightened being, an embodiment of divine love. With such thoughts I could feel warmth spreading through me.

    As we climbed upwards into those enchanting valleys where the rushing river, Mother Ganga, snakes her way downwards, the sheer beauty of these regions overwhelmed me. It was hypnotic. Swamiji once said that divine love is the ultimate hypnosis. One loses oneself completely into the

The Serpent Rising

Beloved. Was I just frightened of letting go, of loving?

By the time we reached the hanging bridge of Laxman Jhula and had begun our trek up to the ashram, my heart was thumping with both fear and excitement. When we reached the ashram gate with its towering spikes and the central emblem of three pink lotus flowers, I waited for Angus to catch up with the keys. As I stood there looking up the hill, a very strange feeling came over me. Tingling sensations, like tiny explosions, were spreading across my forehead and over the top of my head. These sensations were not unpleasant or painful. Rather I was feeling an enormous release as if a boulder had been lifted out of my mind; all that pressure from thinking and doubting so much. For the first time in months a lightness and softness came over me. I could not resist it.

When I reached the third bend in the spiralling path I stopped for a few moments and gazed at Ganga rushing below me, pushing her way through the rocks at the rapids to leap freely past them. This glorious river never ceased to enthral me, ever dancing but ever the same Ganga. Her sound was like a continuous *Om*, the sacred sound of the yogis and when I listened, her sound seemed to be inside me as well, deep within my heart. Surely this river is the most sacred, the most cherished river in the world. Hindus believe that to bathe in her pure waters will wash away the state of sin. I had also been told that scientists have discovered that she is physically pure because bacteria counts are extraordinarily low.

I could hear Angus puffing as he struggled up the steep path with some provisions — lentils, rice, flour and kerosene — that we had purchased in

Rishikesh. Angus had insisted that he carry this load up by himself. Perhaps he thought he could work off extra *karma* by being such a martyr. I was left to carry my light shoulder bag. Angus and I had hardly uttered a word to each other since leaving Delhi more than six hours before. I suspected that he thought he would be infected with my negativity, or that Swamiji had instructed him not to talk to me.

But I wasn't feeling so negative now. I glanced back and noticed the festering sores on Angus's legs, his swollen knees and his thin skeletal body. He really needed to see a doctor but he obviously thought he was purifying himself and the sores were toxins being eliminated. I shuddered. Why did Swamiji treat the boys like slaves and yet treat us girls so well, at least on a physical level? Why was there so much secret about our sexual dalliances? In *satsang* Swamiji often preached the virtues of celibacy for yoga aspirants and yet the boys appeared to be oblivious to what went on behind closed doors during the day and sometimes during the night. There was too much about this yogi that didn't make sense.

As I walked towards the veranda door, Swamiji moved from behind the curtain, his bright orange robe trailing behind him. He tilted his head to one side, screwed up his nose and smiled at me. The expression on his face for some reason reminded me of Rasputin. I told myself to be careful and to not look into his eyes. I did not want him hypnotising me. I took a deep breath and strode towards him. 'I can't stay, Swamiji. I have to catch the train back to Delhi. Can I have my mail?'

He stood there, lifted his chin up slightly and laughed. The red *tilak* he had drawn on his forehead looked like a sword rather than a flame. His hand tugged at his thin, straggly beard. 'Nonsense! The Delhi train doesn't leave for many hours. Why are you always running away from me, Archana? Will you never learn? There is nothing outside. It's all just a dream. Have you forgotten the love I have for you and our divine *sangams*? Have you forgotten the meaning of your name already? Your *sadhana* is to be like Archana, the goddess of worship, not Mary who drags you into Hell all the time.'

I cringed. I could think of nothing to say. I felt like a little girl and began to wonder what he really meant by outside. He surely couldn't mean outside this ashram as if this place were the centre of the universe. If 'outside' meant the mind seeking satisfaction through the body and the senses then it shouldn't matter where in the world I was because I'd still be carrying my mind, here or there. I didn't dare ask him because I knew from past experience that when I asked such questions, he'd retort in a sarcastic tone that my clever intellect was my greatest barrier to faith, to finding out the truth about things. He just expected me to listen and not question.

Angus walked past me, knelt down and kissed Swamiji's feet. He then walked towards the Kriya Room. Swamiji beamed. 'See! What faith! Like a diamond. Die mind. Why do you fear the power of faith? Go inside and wait. There is something I want to give you.'

I went inside and sat down on a thick cotton rug on the concrete floor. I rested my back against the inside wall and looked outside. The heavy braided curtains were pulled back, held in place by old clothes pegs that clung through the cloth onto the diamond-shaped meshes. I could smell the jasmine flowers that were growing near the water tank about 50 metres away. A dove called out to its mate. Its call was soon returned. Their sounds pierced me, entering deep within. The sound of Ganga in the distance also soothed me. Swamiji had often remarked that sounds such as these were sounds of the soul.

Swamiji was now moving up and down the length of the veranda, first lighting incense, then rearranging some flowers on the *puja* place and pouring *ghee* into one of the lamps. He then moved across to the curtains, released some of them and pulled them across. He performed each action as if he was totally absorbed in each task, fully in the present moment, concentrated. I rested my head on my knees, which were hunched up close to me. The cramping and tingling sensations in my head were growing stronger. I sighed and closed my eyes. I sat there and wished I could just slip into a deep peaceful sleep and never wake up. I felt so tired, worn out by my wretched life, my restless mind.

I was aroused a few moments later by Anand Kirti. Anand was a *sannyasin* from Germany and a devotee of Bhagwan Rajneesh in Poona and had come recently to the ashram to study hatha yoga for a few months. He had brought me a stainless steel glass of hot *tulsi chai*, my favourite. He smiled at me and I smiled back. I liked the look of him — he looked down to earth yet impish — and I wondered what on earth he was doing in this crazy place. I left the glass of *chai* next to the wall, as it was still too hot to grip around the bottom. After Anand had gone out of the veranda, Swamiji came and stood near me. His toes crept out from his robe and he began stroking my feet. I remembered Sai Baba doing the same thing. Swamiji was holding onto a piece of paper.

'Archana, do you remember the application form you filled out when you first came here?' He handed it to me. It seemed years and years since I had filled it out. After the question, 'What do you want to learn here?' I read my answer, 'I want to understand the truths behind this existence, the meaning of life and who I am.'

What an absurd answer that was, I thought. Now all I wanted was to be able to live in the world without being affected by its pace and pressures. I wanted to be able to live anywhere and to find some direction in my life. Swamiji was waiting for me to finish reading. Then he went on, 'Well, now I'm going to give you what you wanted. What you really have been looking for. All the questions you've been asking all your life will be answered. All your confusion will be explained.' Inwardly, I groaned.

The tingling sensations in my head were getting stronger, like electric currents passing through my brain. I did not resist them for they were not at all painful. I felt myself letting go, giving in. I then became conscious of a pool of energy vibrating somewhere at the top of my head. Then in some strange way I felt as if the top of my head was open: that there was now a hole in it through which the electric currents passed. It was the most extraordinary sensation. My head became an empty vehicle for electric currents. Joy began to well up in me. I began to feel an ecstasy and my heart and stomach felt warm. My mouth kept opening and closing gently.

I turned around. Swamiji was standing near the veranda door and looking up into the sky. He was smiling blissfully. There was no solid outline to his physical body. It had become fuzzy and there was now a bright, white light surrounded him. I stared in disbelief. I had never seen anything like this. Here I was looking at a divine god-like being, yet hours previously I had decided he was dangerous, probably demonic. Swamiji then turned around and winked at me. He did not say anything but walked over to his bedroom door. But rather than walking, he seemed to be floating about six inches off the ground. He opened the door and glided inside. The door was then shut and bolted and soon I could see through the window the glow of light from a candle. Then the smell of rose incense drifted through.

    I looked out through the veranda and saw Anand Kirti and Angus moving around outside the kitchen. I watched them walk over to the tank and collect some buckets of water. They then squatted outside the kitchen and began to wash some dishes with ash, coconut husk and water. I began to laugh in sheer delight. They looked like robots moving around, their movements mechanical, jerky, indecisive. It was as if I was looking right through them and seeing them from another level of consciousness. As I watched them and laughed, I looked and noticed that my body was now surrounded by white light similar to the one surrounding Swamiji. Sometimes Anand and Angus would glance over at me sitting on the veranda but they were apparently unaware of what was happening to me, or that I was in some way different from them. But as I watched them I realised I had woken up and that they were still asleep. I now knew what Swamiji meant when he talked to us about the spiritual states of sleep, dream and being awake. Awakened, I felt that I myself was god-like, a divine being.

Some time later I became conscious that I was standing outside my body and looking down at it. It was as if I had X-ray vision because I could see right through it. When I focused on my brain I noticed that it was no longer solid (a mass of matter), but actually a network of electrical circuits, many of which were twisted and fused. I then became aware that Swamiji was sitting in full lotus position far away in the night sky and I was up near him. From his fingertips I saw streams of energy, like lightning bolts rocketing down onto the earth, onto the ashram and entering my brain into which I could still see. These lightning streaks were hitting the circuits in my brain trying to mend them so that the energy could flow more freely through them.

Swamiji then disappeared and I began to hear a deep voice booming. 'Your journey is to be in touch with this flow, this flow of divine love. When you are in touch with this flow everything you need will come to you. In reality nothing exists but this divine love. This is your real home, the creation of love. All else is a dream your mind is creating. Your soul is old and tired. You have been searching for a long, long time, many lifetimes, for your real home. All things that you feel in your heart are to remind you of your real nature, which is divine love.'

I felt as if my heart was going to break. Tears were streaming down my face. I didn't try to hold them back or wipe them away. These tears seemed to be coming from somewhere deep inside of me, an endless source of sorrow: the sorrow of my soul in separation from its source. It was then I realised I was back in my body, and sitting on the floor in front of the *puja* place. Fresh, burning coals had been placed on the *barossi*. When I looked down at my hands they were still surrounded by white light. My eyes were wide open and unblinking; my eyeballs felt as if they were made of transparent, satin-like jelly with light pouring through them. I felt separate from my body though at the same time I was conscious of somehow being in it.

Suddenly fragments of my life flashed before me but instead of imagining these inside my head, they were being projected outside of me: reels and reels of film, pictures of my searching and my running away, my grasping, my identifying with my body and especially with the pain in my head.

The voice then began booming again. 'The whole world is contained within you. Your mind is just projecting it outside. In reality none of this exists; there is no world, no mind. There is no thought, no emotion. There is only bliss and ecstasy.' Then scenes flashed before me: scenes I had experienced with Sai Baba, with Goenka at the Vipassana camp and with Swamiji. It was like a movie of the past year in fast motion, flashing before my eyes. All the devotion as well as all my doubts and negativity resurfaced. The negativity that had blocked the flow of divine energy causing pain and confusion.

Then these three beings, each of whom I had at some stage accepted as my teacher, appeared before me and I was looking directly into the faces of Sai Baba and Goenka as well as Swamiji. I then felt a searing pain in my chest as if a knife had been plunged into it and these three figures suddenly merged together, transformed into a large mass of luminous light that came towards me and was sucked into my heart. A few seconds later the deep sound of a beautiful *bhajan* being sung by Sai Baba blasted through the night sky. This was followed by Goenka's deep Pali chant booming towards me. Lastly came Swamiji's chanting of a Vedic *mantra*, my favourite:

Om kayena vacha mana sendriyava
buddyat manava prakritir syavabhad
karomi yadyad sakalam parasmai
narayani ti samaypyami

Which means in short: 'Oh God, I surrender my intellect to you.'

These sounds suddenly increased in speed, became gibberish until they were like a cackle, a burst of hysterical laughter. Then the sounds started whooshing towards me and disappeared inside of me. I started laughing and noticed Swamiji moving out of his bedroom. He walked slowly up to the *puja* place with some candles in one hand and replaced those that had almost burnt out. I wanted to reach over and rest my head on his feet and kiss his toes but found I couldn't move. He looked at me out of the corner of his eye and said sweetly, 'Enjoying the divine creation of Archana?' He walked swiftly back into his room, and closed the door. He looked like the god Krishna.

I began laughing hysterically. I was creating my life's drama and my crazy search for a guru and 'enlightenment'. I had projected these gurus myself! I had created these gurus that I had been clutching onto or rejecting. In reality they don't exist. In reality nothing exists except an ocean of divine love.

All at once everything seemed to make sense. I began to realise that my whole life up to this time was an absurd joke. I was always running and hiding and changing my mind. My intellect with its doubting and questioning had been my greatest barrier.

I looked outside again and even though it was evening, everything was luminous and dancing in light: the flowers, the trees, the clouds and the sky. The jungle and world around me were no longer solid; they were a moving enchanting vibration of light. Through the skies, the sound of *Om* boomed and echoed and merged with the wind whispering, the trees swaying and the sound of Ganga. These sounds and this almighty sound of *Om* seemed to be inside me too. There was no separation from the world and my heart was connected with the universe.

I was now completely alone. There were no gurus being projected, no film strips of my life. I was alone and overflowing with love, completely happy and content. Some time later I left my body again and felt myself being propelled through space at a breathtaking speed. Suddenly I wasn't in this world anymore. I had transcended time and space and was being dragged up to this bright white river of light into which the universe and the sound of *Om* were disappearing. I yearned to disappear into this light, to rest at last. I began to feel myself disappearing, into nothingness.

At some stage I panicked and fear emerged. For there was a part of me that did not want to disappear, to lose myself. A tug of war began. A desire to stay alive, conscious and remain on earth began to drag me downwards, yet the part of me yearning to merge into this light was pulling me in another direction. This tug-of-war went on for what seemed ages but I had by this time lost all conception of time. Then I felt myself being yanked downwards and I suddenly found myself back in my body, which was sitting in front of the *puja* place. I knew I wasn't ready. I wasn't ready for this state of 'enlightenment'. I didn't want to see any more. All my questions had been answered. Then everything went blank.

I have no recollection of what happened in the hours that followed and only remember being conscious of the morning arriving with the sun rising and the birds singing. My brain felt fused: the most excruciating pains I had ever experienced were raging through it. It felt as if it was on fire. In spite of this physical pain I also felt detached from it and I would keep lapsing back into orgasmic states of pure ecstasy with my mouth opening and shutting gently. Sometimes I would sigh, involuntarily.

Angus walked passed me and mumbled 'Hari Om'. I was surprised that he didn't say anything about the state I was in. Surely I looked different? Didn't he see that I was divine now? I stood up and began to move slowly. My body felt as if it was made of light and I couldn't stop myself smiling.

Later that morning I went for a jungle walk with Swamiji. I felt child-like, full of awe and wonder as I followed this graceful, moving figure — orange like the sun. We walked in silence until we reached a ridge high above the ashram. Down below us Mother Ganga was roaring and rushing over the rapids. Temple bells were ringing and echoing up through the valley. Conches were sounding and calling, drums could be heard beating. It was time for midday *puja* in the many temples of Swargashram and Laxman Jhula. We stood and watched a brilliantly plumed peacock on a nearby hillock raise its head in the air and strut around to begin a mating dance.

Swamiji winked at me, 'You know about Krishna and Radha now? Last night you would have tasted what divine love is really like.' Unable to speak, I knelt down and kissed his toes and rested my head on his feet. My brain was still searing with heat and piecing pains. But they did not bother me for on this day I truly felt as if I was divine and Swamiji was my beloved, my God.

When I finally spoke about my extraordinary experience, I was astonished that Swamiji did not know the details of what had occurred. 'I just plugged you into the centre of the Cosmos, into your own divine creation. I took the risk of doing this to prevent you from running away again and plunging into worldliness. You were not ready to experience such higher consciousness. You could have easily died from the voltage. At one stage you were dying and beginning to leave your body but I used my *prana* to drag you back again. One day you will understand everything.'

Later on that day I wrote to my parents to tell them that I would be spending the rest of my life on the Himalayan Hill. Something extraordinary had happened to me, something that they might find difficult to understand or believe. I had woken up in the Divine creation of Love and seen for a fact that Swamiji was a being in the order of Gautama the Buddha and Jesus the Christ. My negativity and reactions were just a resistance to the Cosmic flow. Now I could begin to take on their wretched *karma* as well as that of my brother and sister, work it all off in the same way that Swamiji had taken on mine. They were to ignore any of my previous letters sent from Calcutta and Delhi. Now I realised my doubts were poison from my lower mind. Bordering this letter and the envelope it was sealed in, I drew in bright pastels pictures of flowers, snakes, stars and hearts. On the back of the envelope I wrote: 'From Archana, Creation of Love, Himalayan Peaks, Cerebrum of the Earth'. Some weeks later my mother wrote back thanking me for the letter but made no mention of my cosmic experience that I had described in detail to her. Instead she wrote about the weather, Dad's latest aches and pains, the neighbours and the latest book she was reading. It was as if she hadn't got my message, my divine gift.

For months the memory of that night (which had been the third of March, 1974) hovered close to me and constantly reminded me that Swamiji was not a madman when I watched him in one of his fits of rage, his Rudra dance of destruction. I now believed that he was in a permanent state of higher consciousness and always blissful and that his body and mind were instruments only, to be used for the purpose of waking us up. People losing faith or running away no longer disturbed me. I was convinced I had finally come home, that I had reached the end of the journey and there would never be any need to leave the ashram again. I would stay there for the rest of my life and die there an old lady. There was now no need to test myself or to prove the authenticity or usefulness of Swamiji's teachings. At times I would even lapse back into the states of consciousness I had experienced that night and was refilled with ecstasy and love.

For over seven months I experienced intense pains and heat in my head and sometimes up through my spinal column. Several times a day I would retreat back to the Shakti Kutir to lie down on the hard wooden cot and place wet cloths over my face and around my head. Sometimes I would slip off my robe and slide down into the water tank. It became impossible for me to perform even the simplest of tasks beyond a certain point. Even sweeping the veranda for more than a few minutes at a time would be overwhelming. I would suddenly feel as if my brain had changed gear and had begun to speed up, faster and faster until it was if the machinery inside was going to break down. It seemed as if the wires of the circuits in my brain had begun to cross each other and were burning themselves out. Tasks that required conscious, analytical thought such as writing letters, reading, doing the office accounts would bring this condition on quicker than anything else. The more I tried to resist it or ignore it, the worse I felt and the longer it would take for me to recover. Some days I would have to go and lie down for two to three hours at a time. Hatha yoga sometimes worked, as it seemed to bring the energy down out of my head and disperse it through other parts of my body. But water more than anything else eased the pain and the fire inside.

During the summer heat I would often go down to Ganga to recover from one of these attacks. Sitting by her side I would breathe in the coldness of her melting glacial waters. Sometimes I would take down jasmine flowers, throw them out one by one. The water would pick them up, they would race along and then slowly disappear and in the distance they would look like glistening stars. I'd often lie on my back on the soft, white sand, close my eyes and listen to the sound of the water rising and falling and fading away. The sound would wash through me like a chain of Oms reverberating. Here there was no need of *mantras*. The river had a wordless one of her own, a primeval sound.

I learned to ignore the smells of human faeces, the blobs of brown caked on the rocks and around the shore. For the banks of this sacred river was also the 'toilet' for the *sadhus*, swamis and pilgrims who came near her or lived close by. As well as drinking the water they not only wash their clothes in it but also their bodies (including their behinds after toileting). At times I would turn my head and catch a glimpse of a *sadhu* or a swami peeping from behind one of the rocks. They looked like foxes watching their prey. Some had brown shaven heads, others matted dreadlocks and all had vermilion smeared across their foreheads. Presumably they were waiting for me to slip off my clothes and enter the water naked and no doubt had seen other foreigners doing this. But I had learnt the way of Indian women: the way of discretion. After pulling my long petticoat up over my breasts and tying it tightly with the waist cord, I would then unravel my sari, unbutton my *choli* blouse and pull it off, and enter the water in my petticoat.

Sitting near the flowing waters of this mighty river I wrote poems — poems for my Beloved One, our union and our separation. Swamiji called me his heart and said that in his subtle body I was his heart *chakra*. I wrote poems about the third of March and disappearing into the silent stillness and ecstasy of love.

During the hot summer months, I slept with Swamiji on the roof. The days were longer now and instead of hot-spiced *chai* we preferred cold, *lassi* drinks made from Ganga water, curd, sugar and mint leaf all whisked together. I loved this season in India when the world became hazily dream-like.

Following this summer languor, the wet season arrived with her blankets of rain. The ground absorbed the wetness and released new life: bright, rich greenness in the wild jungle and brilliant orange, yellow and white flowers in the ashram gardens. Rainbows often arched across the skies and steam rose and danced over the hills.

Things were quiet in the ashram now and Swamiji often left the down-side gate locked during visiting time. A notice would be hung over the lock to say that there was no visiting for that day. The wet season also seemed to release unknown creativity within the few of us that now resided in the ashram. Each day we spent many hours painting, drawing or writing and we were constantly amazed by the beauty and skill of our work. It was as if we were not doing this work ourselves. Rather it was flowing through us. As months passed, the pain and heat in my head slowly began to ebb and I could spend longer reading and writing.

I grew close to Anand Kirti, who was altogether different from anyone I had known here. He claimed that his guru, Rajneesh, in Poona had sent him up to the Himalayas to practise hatha yoga. I was surprised that Swamiji had even given him permission to stay here because he wore orange clothes, the garb of *sannyasins* and also said his name was Swami Anand Kirti, though we were not allowed to call him 'Swami'. Evidently all the followers of Rajneesh (who was called the sex guru throughout India) were called '*Swamis*' if they were male devotees, and '*Mas*' ('Ma' being short for 'Mataji') for female devotees. Kirti used to practise strange

meditations, which had probably developed out of Western psychoanalytic thought.
One seemed particularly bizarre. It was called dynamic mediation. In this meditation Anand used to go into the Circle and jump up and down and shout out 'hoo, hoo', while waving his arms up and down. The tight curls of his long black hair would swing out in all directions and at times he seemed to be out of control, taken over in a wild frenzy. All the meditations I had learnt involved sitting down and keeping the body still in an attempt to slow down the mind. Anand explained to me that this dynamic meditation was only done in the morning soon after one had woken up as it was designed to shake one out of a *tamasic* (sluggish) state and release energies for the day ahead. He further explained that there were other Rajneesh meditations that could be used at other times of the days for different purposes. When I remembered how often meditators at the Vipassana camp fell asleep for long periods or even how some of the aspirants here dozed off during meditation sessions there seemed to be some sense in this strange dynamic meditation Anand practised. I used to watch him and wish I could go out into the Circle and shout out 'hoo', shake around and dance with him.
Swamiji often ridiculed Kirti about some of his practices and also for wearing an orange robe and *mala* with a picture of Rajneesh on it. But Kirti didn't seem to mind. I enjoyed him being here as he was the only person apart from Swamiji whom I could talk to and who was friendly with me. All the others seemed to get lost in their own little worlds, in their obsessions with Swamiji as their guru.
Towards the end of the year as things began to

settle down inside me I began to reflect on that fateful night — the night that Swamiji and I began to call the Third of March. There was no possibility that the experience could have been induced by drugs because at no stage beforehand did I take anything to eat or drink. The glass of *chai* that Anand Kirti had brought me had been left against the wall untouched all night. Further, I couldn't even imagine Swamiji giving us drugs — and from where would he have got them? Then perhaps he had hypnotised me in some way. But I had scarcely looked Swamiji in the eyes all evening and most of the time I was acutely aware of my physical surroundings, which is not typical of someone in a hypnotic state. The only conclusion I could reach was that Swamiji had (through his yogic powers) connected me directly to the Cosmos, which is exactly what he said he had done.

Chapter 9

Births and Deaths

Months passed and I realised that the Third of March had changed me. I no longer wanted to leave. But other aspirants kept coming and going for various reasons.

Anand Kirti left in October to go back to Poona to Rajneesh. As he was about to leave, we stood outside the veranda and waited for Swamiji to come and give him his blessings. Kirti held my hands. 'I'll see you in Poona sometime, Archana. You don't belong here.'

'One never knows. But at this time I can't imagine ever leaving this place. Swamiji needs me to look after him.' I heard a rustle of the curtain behind me and turned around. Swamiji was peering at me with a strange look on his face: his Rasputin look. He stepped out and in his hand was a small silver *catori* of *tilak*. He placed his fingertip into the mixture and dabbed a red spot on Anand Kirti's forehead. Kirti knelt down and touched Swamiji's feet while Swamiji rested his outstretched right hand on top of Kirti's head for a few moments.

Swamiji and I watched him walk down the path. He paused at the flagpoles and waved at us, calling out 'Hari Om'. He was one of the few aspirants to leave on good terms with Swamiji and while here he had not 'freaked out' the way other boys did. Perhaps this was because he already had another guru. His faith in Rajneesh had been unwavering during his time here yet he still respected Swamiji as his yoga teacher. Kirti was the only person at the ashram who had been friendly to me and I felt sad to see him go. I was going to miss many things about him, especially his dynamic meditation in the Circle each morning.

Later that evening while I was combing Swamiji's hair he looked at me in the mirror. 'Anand Kirti infect you with his Rajneesh talk? That trip is kindergarten level in the ocean of the world. You are past all that free sex and psychic infection. Those Rajneesh swamis are just pretend swamis. They have no right to wear orange.'

A week after Kirti had left, Michel arrived back from France. He had earned enough money to stay up to two years depending on whether the Indian government granted him sufficient extension visas. I was lucky in this respect because visitors from British Commonwealth countries did not require visas to stay in India. Swamiji said it was our good *karma*. Most of the people who stayed at the ashram had to fill in pages of applications to extend their visas and sometimes had to go down to Delhi to lodge them. When their requests were not granted they had to leave the country for at least six months before they could return. The only other long-term aspirants who did not have these visa hassles were Angus and two Australian girls, Dhyana and Santwana who were close friends. I had not yet met them though they had evidently been somewhere in the ashram that day I returned with Deborah to collect my belongings. They had also stayed before I had first arrived here and often spent periods in Japan teaching English.

During the first week Michel was back here, I noticed him and Swamiji whispering a lot. Every afternoon they went for a jungle walk together. Then in the second week Michel left one afternoon while I was away taking a bath in Ganga. When I asked Swamiji why Michel had gone he became angry. 'Don't ask me such questions. It's none of your business. Keep your mind on your *sadhana* practices.' A few weeks later when I went to the post-office to collect the mail, I noticed on the back of one envelope Michel's name, with an address in Melbourne, Australia. As soon as Swamiji read the letter he locked himself in his bedroom for several days. He had little to eat and the little food he did eat he went out and prepared himself. The gates were closed downside and the 'No Visitors' sign hung over one of the spikes. Once when Swamiji walked past me to go to the kitchen he snarled, 'Go away. I don't want your curiosity vibrations poisoning my food.' I laughed to myself, thinking that if he had made such a comment to me a year ago I would have been devastated and run around the back to pack my bags.

As Swamiji had stopped taking *satsang* classes and overseeing our chores, I took over the running of the ashram, especially the cooking and preparation of food. Things were peaceful without Swamiji's 'teacher' lurking around reprimanding us, yet I still felt ill at ease. I guessed Swamiji was tuning into some female devotee and trying to help her as he had tried to do with me when I was running around Delhi and Calcutta. Probably it was one or both of the Australian girls.

Finally Swamiji came out of his room. I knew from his expression that his mood had changed. He asked for some *elaichi chai* and when I brought it to him, he smiled and rubbed his forefingers together: 'Want some of this later?' I smiled. I had missed him holding me, missed the feel of his velvet-like skin and the entering of his energy. He then went on, 'One of my beloveds has rejected me. She has got caught up in worldly life. You will leave me one day too and never return.'

'No, I won't, Swamiji. I will never leave you. How can you say such a thing?' Even though I could understand why people left and never returned, it still puzzled me why Swamiji appeared to be so attached to his disciples. Why couldn't they come back of their own volition? But then I realised I would not have been back here if Swamiji had not sent Angus to Delhi to find me. And then I would not have experienced the Third of March.

Swamiji seldom seemed concerned when any of the boys left or ran away. A few days after Swamiji's retreat, Angus left sometime during the night. The following morning Swamiji was amused. 'Pig's gone to wallow in the mud of the world, in *maya*. And Michel the horse has decided to gallop around Australia for a while. Things are much more peaceful when the boys leave. All they think about is food. They are all so sleepy.' He then screwed up his face and squinted, 'And what about you, Archana? You don't want to leave any more, do you? You are no longer the little mouse you used to be. Running and hiding everywhere. You are much stronger now and more powerful. We will have to look for another animal name for you.' I hoped he would choose a name of something beautiful and gentle — a dove or gazelle for instance.

Apart from all these comings and goings, other Westerners came and stayed for short periods. Most were in their twenties, though occasionally an older person stayed. Apart from Western seekers, a servant would be hired and fired usually within a month; some lasted only a day or two. I couldn't understand why we needed servants because we managed to cope with all the work without them and whenever we did have a servant Swamiji treated them worse than the boys. He used to hit and shout abuse at them. He would even give them leftover food that was sometimes a day or so old and had not been kept cool as we had no fridge. To disguise any unpleasant smell, he would spice it heavily. There were always disagreements when Swamiji came to pay them. Swamiji would say that they all were very low human beings and that their gross vibrations reflected on his sensitive and pure body and made him ill.

A letter arrived from Angus a few weeks after his night flight. He was back in Ireland and hoped Swamiji would forgive him. He wrote that he couldn't cope outside and wanted to return as soon as possible, when he had earned enough money. Devotional letters kept coming from Saraswati. She planned to return towards the end of the year. I was not looking forward to her coming back as I had become used to being the chief disciple. I enjoyed taking over the running of the ashram whenever Swamiji shut himself away in his bedroom or whenever he had to leave the ashram to give lectures and talks in Hindi at other ashrams in the district. When Saraswati returned, she would no doubt try to usurp my new position. Neither was I keen on the idea of Swamiji sharing his bed with anyone else. When I had first arrived the notion of Swamiji sleeping with others, to raise their energy, had not bothered me but now that my love for him had grown, I wanted him to myself and did not want to share him.

My greatest fear was that someone else would take my place as chief beloved, as had happened in the past with other consorts. They too had their times of glory and power. I knew Saraswati's time had passed. But would anyone follow me? Occasionally I fantasised about Swamiji becoming an ordinary householder and then we could get married and live a normal life.

Between the rainy season and the cold winter, an interlude of a few months of glorious weather descended on the Himalayan Hill. There was never any rain now, the sky was always clear, the air cool. During these months we practised hatha yoga on the roof most days and resumed the practice of the more difficult cleansing *kriyas*. Swamiji decided he wanted to play with more of the things of the world and so electricity was at last installed in the ashram. This made life much easier as we no longer had to light up kerosene lamps at night. We also purchased a plug-in stove with two elements, which meant the fire did not have to be kept burning all day. We still used the old mud stove for most of the cooking as it was cheaper and because electricity was often cut off without warning and remained off for hours and sometimes days. A telephone was also installed in Swamiji's bedroom. The monthly charges for our food and accommodation were increased from 300 rupees a month to 450 rupees.

In December, Saraswati returned. She came back

laden with presents for Swamiji including a clock, a radio, a tape recorder and clothing. As I had feared she immediately began taking over the duties I become used to doing: serving Swamiji, making his *chai* and tidying his bedroom. I not only resented her taking charge but also the way she treated me like a younger sister. To prevent a major conflict between us, Swamiji decided that each morning we were to both report to him so he could allocate us different chores for the day. He also began to become more discreet about our bedroom liaisons and told me he did not want to upset her. Even though he insisted that he was no longer sleeping with Saraswati, I was not convinced. Sometimes she was called to his bedroom so he could dictate a letter to her for typing and on these occasions she would stay inside for an hour at least. Anything could have happened. But I still believed I was his chief beloved, his heart. Swamiji used to call Saraswati his flower of wisdom and said that in his subtle body she was his head *chakra*. I was content to be his flower of love, his heart *chakra*. I wanted love not wisdom.

Saraswati and I began to get on better but there was a part of me that never trusted her or felt comfortable with her. I didn't regard her as a friend but someone I had to learn to get on with. During visiting times we would sometimes go to Ganga for a swim or for jungle walks or we would stay in her room. She often spoke about her beloved Lord Shiva and claimed that she had been high for the whole year in America. The world did not bother her at all; it was all Shiva's playground, she liked to say. Being outside and away from the ashram did not affect her the way it did me. She also said she would not be able to cope being here in the ashram if she regarded Swamiji as a beloved. For her, he was her guru who could connect her to God, to Shiva. She told me stories about her past as a drug addict in New York and on the drug trail around India for two years and claimed that she was close to death when she first struggled up to the ashram to see Swamiji three years previously. Within two months of carrying out a rigid regime of cleansing *kriyas* and fasting she had apparently cleansed her body thoroughly enough to free herself of drug cravings forever.

But no sooner had things begun to settle down again after Saraswati's return and we had got used to working amicably together, than I began to feel sick on and off during the day and night. Nausea would come over me and I often vomited after eating food that was highly spiced. Swamiji reassured me saying my body was just purifying itself. He advised me to go on a bland diet of mostly fruit, boiled vegetables and yoghurt. I began to get cravings for tomatoes and white toast and so whenever Jorgen went to the market place he would bring back some for me. In spite of this change of diet, the sickness continued.

After about a month the thought that I might be pregnant occurred to me. Swamiji laughed when I suggested this. 'It is not possible. I am in control of your *karma*. Be patient. The sickness will pass.' I hadn't had my period for what seemed ages now but this had never been of great concern to me. Since coming to India and becoming a vegetarian, my periods had been irregular and months would pass without one. In an attempt to rid myself of this sickness, I began to do *kunjal kriya* every morning before drinking *chai*. After quickly drinking one or two litres of warm salty water, I would retch it all up, sometimes with the help of my fingers down my throat. But this did not help and I began to worry that maybe I had cancer. Two more months passed. By now I was convinced something was wrong and decided to go to Rishikesh to see a lady doctor even though Swamiji thought I was being foolish and lacked faith in him.

The doctor's verdict after a quick examination was that not only was I pregnant but also had already passed the early stages. At first I didn't believe her and asked for a blood or urine test but she said that that wasn't necessary as the foetus could be clearly felt in my womb. She also said that I was probably suffering from slight malnutrition.

In a daze I walked out of the clinic and made my way down to the banks of the Ganges. As the news sunk in, a sense of awe and wonder came over me. I was carrying the child of an enlightened being! How about that! I wondered what Swamiji's reaction would be. For hours I sat on the soft white sand and gazed into the swirling waters rushing past. A calmness had come over me and I sat there thinking about what my options were.

I could return alone to New Zealand and have the child there. I could have the child here and live with Swamiji in the ashram, hopefully as husband and wife. Or I could persuade Swamiji to leave the Himalayas and come to New Zealand and live with me there. I couldn't bear the thought of leaving India at this time by myself but the real difficulty about staying here would be having enough money to look after a baby properly. The real problem with continuing to live at the ashram would be that when his wealthy Indian devotees found out about our child they would stop their regular donations. I would have to talk to Swamiji. Perhaps he already knew I was pregnant but hadn't told me because he didn't want me to get rid of it. That made sense.

Some fresh red and yellow flowers streamed past in the water followed by pieces of black debris, the remains of a body recently burnt on a funeral pyre upstream. Death and birth — intertwined threads. Somebody had been plucked from the flow of life into death. One life had finished and another was just beginning. Beginning inside of me.

Saraswati was the first to meet me as I walked up the path. On hearing the news her eyes widened. 'You've got to go straight to Delhi. Tonight. You have to have an abortion. I know a place to go to.' I was stunned. 'Don't be stupid. I wouldn't consider having an abortion.' I charged past her and went straight to Swamiji's room where he was lying down.

His reaction was quite unexpected. He looked embarrassed and uncomfortable, yet I had felt sure that he would have known. I believed he knew everything. 'It's just your bad *karma* catching up with you. An ashram is not the place for a screaming baby.' He was silent for a few seconds and then said: 'You could always go and live in the far-side *kutir*.'

I couldn't believe his reaction and sat there, stunned, until at last he said, 'Go talk to Saraswati. She is worldly-wise. She is the expert in these matters.' But Saraswati was adamant. When I suggested having the baby and probably stay on living here, she became hysterical. 'You'll destroy everything. What about Swamiji's reputation as a swami or a yogi? It would be ridiculous. And what about me? You're just dreaming if you imagine that you could keep the child anywhere. You have to get rid of it.

You have no other choice.' For the rest of the day she locked herself in the room and refused to come out. Sometimes she let out loud screams and you could hear her stamping her feet, pounding her fists against the wall and throwing things.

I could not think clearly and felt totally alone and confused. Swamiji was strangely aloof. I stayed awake most of the night, curled up on my cot in the Shakti Kutir.

The following morning Saraswati still did not come out of her room. She let out wailing noises and the occasional scream throughout the morning. Swamiji blamed me for upsetting her.

I spent most of the day by myself. Most of my life I had looked forward to having a child and yet now I wondered whether perhaps I wasn't stable enough. I definitely wasn't financially secure. I had no income to bring up a child and hated the thought of going back into the world to find a job. I also began to worry about all the things, including *kriyas*, I had done to my body to try and get rid of what I had thought was an illness. The doctor had also said I was under-nourished. Did this mean the baby would have suffered or been damaged in some way?

Saraswati emerged from her room late in the afternoon. Swamiji was still in his bedroom and I had sneaked into the kitchen to make some *chai* and have a snack. The boys had not yet returned from Rishikesh where Swamiji had sent them earlier in the day with a long list of provisions to purchase. Saraswati's eyes were red and swollen. Seeing me next door to her in the kitchen she yelled out that if I didn't leave immediately and have an abortion she would be the one who would leave and never come back. She also said no one would ever come and stay at the ashram again and I would ruin Swamiji's life. I didn't answer her and took my glass of warm *chai* back to my *kutir*.

After one week of indecision and conflicting emotions I realised Saraswati might be right. The situation was hopeless. I couldn't talk to anyone and felt so alone. The boys didn't know what was going on. Swamiji had been ignoring me most of the time. Saraswati remained furious with me and kept insisting that I go to Delhi. It was obvious that if I kept the baby I was going to get no support at all from Swamiji and I would never be allowed to stay at the ashram. I felt bewildered.

Finally, when I asked Saraswati for the address of the hospital she remarked quite nonchalantly, 'I had an abortion there two years ago.' I was stunned and presumed it was Swamiji's child. I didn't dare ask her how many other girls had had abortions. Once I had made the decision to have an abortion my mind was more peaceful. I just cut out any thoughts about what lay ahead. I went to Delhi on the night-train and was admitted to the hospital the next morning.

The doctor who performed my initial examination was abrupt and unsympathetic. She was a large lady with short-cropped hair and she had no kumkum spot that Indian ladies usually wear on their foreheads. She thumped me on my back several times and called me 'hippy' instead of Archana. As I was dressing she sat there watching me. 'Why do you pretend to be a *sadhu*? *Sadhus* don't get pregnant.' Without waiting for a reply, she continued, 'I am a Christian and it would be better if you adopted the religion of your home country. Hinduism is an inferior religion and many sects practise devil worship. Many of these gurus are crooks.' I didn't answer. I was on the verge of breaking down.

She continued, 'You are very advanced. Five months, maybe even six months. Almost too late to do anything. Certainly too late for a simple suction aspiration. We are busy here. You will have to wait another fortnight before we can perform the intra-saline method. But if you give me *baksheesh* I can arrange to do it tomorrow. Say 200 rupees.' I took out 20 ten-rupee notes from my wallet and handed them over without looking at her.

The following day I was given a local anaesthetic and an amniotic injection was inserted through the wall of my abdomen. Within twelve hours (I had been told) contractions should begin. I was sent back to my ward and told to rest and wait. In the ward there were about ten other ladies either waiting for or recovering from abortions. They all had friends and relatives with them who either slept on the floor alongside their beds or curled up on the beds themselves. They talked and laughed a lot. None of them appeared to speak English. I decided to ignore them, as I didn't feel like being interrogated.

Hours went by and I felt nothing, not even the slightest movement over my abdomen let alone a contraction. The intra-saline procedure did not work. I was told the only option now was to have an induction. This was scheduled for the following day. I didn't even ask what the procedure entailed. The less I knew about what was going on the better. I just longed for it all to be over so I could return to my Himalayan Hill and to Swamiji. That night I rang Swamiji. I wanted to be brave and strong but burst into tears. He sounded concerned and said he would send Saraswati to be with me until it was all over. He said he was angry with her for not coming down with me in the first place. He also would give her 300 rupees for me. I was so relieved. At last a bit of sympathy. I returned to the ward, climbed into my bed and buried myself under the sheets.

Saraswati arrived early the next morning. The people in the ward all turned their heads and stared at her as she entered with her arms swimming exaggeratedly from side to side and her white robes fluttering. A bright red *tilak* mark in the form of a flame had been drawn right up the centre of the forehead, the way Swamiji used to wear one. Her hair was twisted tightly around in a knot on the top of her head — a Shiva knot characteristic of Shiva renunciates. Intertwined through this knot she had stuck about a dozen fresh jasmine flowers. Several threads of *mala* beads hung around her neck including a *rudraksha* seed around her throat on a string.

Her eyes had that wide staring unblinking look and her eyeballs bulged outwards more than usual. She looked as if she as going off to a wedding or a festive celebration and did not ask me how I was feeling. She began to boast about how wonderful it had been with Swamiji since I had left and all the *samadhi* states she had entered. I buried my head in my hands in disbelief. Her manner abruptly changed. 'Look, pull yourself together. I want to leave soon. Swamiji needs me.'

I looked at her aghast and said Swamiji had told me she should stay until it was all over. She said that was impossible now because after I had rung, Swamiji had become sick and was lying on his bed most of the time trying to work through my terrible *karma*. She sighed. 'So transparent. Just a little child. I often think he doesn't even know what's happening to him. He's just being used as a divine instrument.' I knew she just wanted to return before me to take advantage of Swamiji's attention.

Nothing made sense anymore. I couldn't understand what was happening to me. I couldn't understand why this pregnancy was just my *karma* and not Swamiji's. A nurse came in and said it was time. I felt numb. I was lifted onto a trolley and wheeled away. Saraswati followed. As soon as we reached the doors of the delivery room she put her hands together in prayer position, said 'Hari Om' and walked out. I didn't reply. I lay there and stared up at the white ceiling oblivious to what was going on. Hospital staff were moving here and there around me. I felt a surge of hatred for Saraswati but I realised I had to get my thoughts together before I broke down all together. I knew then that if I didn't hold tightly onto my faith in Swamiji mainly based on what happened on the Third of March, then there was the possibility of my losing my mind altogether. The only thing that would carry me through was my faith. I had to stop being negative and had to believe that an abortion was the right thing to do. I was only doing it for Swamiji's sake. In service to the guru. True surrender.

A drip was inserted into my wrist and the nurse and orderlies left the room. After a few moments I began to feel slight cramping in my lower abdomen. These intensified until it was as if my pelvic and public bones were being wrenched apart with a deep thudding pain. Waves and waves of pain. For hours I lay there and often stared at the tear-like drip that slowly slid down the transparent tube, knowing that at the end of its downward journey there would be more pain. With each drip, the pain intensified. Confusion came over me. I had not been told to expect any pain. I hadn't been told to expect anything. I had not asked. I had given little thought to what was about to happen at all. Sweat was coursing down my face and my thin cotton nightdress was dripping wet.

Finally I could take it no more. I began screaming. A nurse rushed in leaving the door to swing noisily behind her. 'Shut up, you silly girl. We're trying to relax next door. We're in the middle of a card game. It's our break.' Her large body, her podgy face with a smudged red kumkum spot, and *kajal*-rimmed eyes loomed over me. I felt frightened of her. It suddenly occurred to me that perhaps they were trying to kill me. I reached up and tried to pull the drip out of my wrist. The nurse leapt at me and pinned me down as she shouted something in Hindi. Two other nurses rushed in. My wrists were then tied tightly on the rail of the bed head with the drip still attached. One of the nurses snarled, 'It's your *karma*, Anglaisy hippy.' They left the room giggling to themselves.

More hours passed. My lips were dry and parched. I could hear voices laughing and talking in the next room. I called out for some water. Nobody came. I became desperate. I began praying. I prayed to Krishna, the beloved of the *gopis*. I prayed to Shiva sitting in stillness on the top of Mt Kailash. I prayed to my enigmatic boy-yogi of the Himalayan garden. And for good measure, to Jesus and Buddha. I prayed to the little one being wrenched from within me. The pain began to overwhelm me. I began to writhe and twist on the bed. I thought death was near. Suddenly thick wetness spurted and gushed out between my legs. I looked down. There was blood splattered everywhere all over the sheets, my night dress and even across to the far wall. I glanced at the clock on the wall opposite me: I had been in this room for fifteen hours. I shrieked.

One of the nurses strode in. She untied my wrists, took out the drip and lifted up my nightdress. She picked up the foetus and began to dangle it in front of my face. I was mortified. I had expected a rather amorphous lump but this was a tiny human being. She laughed. 'It's a boy, you slut.' She tossed it into a metal bucket and left the room.

I lay there in a state of shock, feeling completely defiled. The abortion was now an act of murder. It was not so simple anymore. I lay there sodden. Blood was still oozing between my legs. Another nurse came in and began cleaning the walls. I lost control. 'Can't you even clean me, you fucking bitch?' Deep sobs and wails heaved through me as I struggled to lift myself out of the bed. My only thought was to run away, get out of this hospital. I passed out.

I came to as I was being wheeled back to the ward. Tears engulfed me again. I felt as if my stomach was going to cave in. Blood was still caked on my feet, which poked out from the end of the white sheets. I had to get out of this place. As I lifted myself up, the world went black again.

Many hours later I stirred to find a woman doctor standing by my bed. She gently stroked my forehead. I burst into tears. She tried to comfort me but I couldn't stop sobbing. I could hear her words washing over me. 'You've had a rough time. There was a lot of resistance. That child obviously didn't want to come out. I wish you had come to us earlier.' Her soft voice brought on more tears of utter anguish. She walked away and I was left alone. I covered my head completely with the bloodstained sheet and cried myself to sleep.

At four o clock the next morning, I dragged myself out of bed, shoved a towel between my legs, grabbed my bag and began to shuffle out of the ward. Everything was quiet, there seemed to be nobody awake. The corridors were dimly lit. Orderlies were curled up asleep on the lino floor in the corridor. As I passed a trolley I grabbed a packet of modess pads from one of the trays and stuffed it in my bag.

As I stumbled out into the heat and the noise of Delhi waking up, the sun was just beginning to climb up into the sky, flashes of red in a distant grey sky. It looked like blood streaking, the blood of birth and sometimes death.

I stood there waiting for a rickshaw or taxi. From a nearby temple I could hear drums beating, cymbals clanging together and a deep voice singing a song used in *arti*, 'Jai, Jagadisha hare ...' The sound seemed far away but also very close. That haunting sound of worship from somewhere deep in my past, long ago. I thought of Swamiji, Ganga and the Himalayas. The sooner I was back there, the sooner I could be healed and would be able to make sense of this nightmare. Everything will be all right, I kept whispering to myself.

Sleeping bodies wrapped in filthy rags were clustered together in groups on the footpath. Some had begun to stir, to drag themselves up and begin their endless scavenging for survival. I turned away, still unable to look at the poverty of India directly in the face.

I used up the equivalent of a month's board at the ashram for a taxi fare home. The driver, tall and thin with oily hair pasted close to his head, sat sideways in his seat for most of the way. He wore a khaki safari suit and chain-smoked the hand-rolled *beedi* cigarettes. He kept looking at me and chattering away to me in faltering English. I hardly listened. I felt weak and dizzy. I pleaded with him to stop pressing his hand on the horn, an addiction of Indian drivers. They sound their horn even when there is nothing on the road. Every so often when his head was turned away I'd lean forwards, remove the bloody pad from between my legs and replace it with a clean one. I'd wrap the sodden ones in newspapers and push them into the bag at my feet. My remaining strength was spent fingering my sandalwood beads and chanting to myself, 'Om Nama Shivayaa' over and over in rounds of 108. It was the only drug I had. It helped. My mind slowly became blank, numbed.

I felt sure that after returning to the ashram, life would return to normal and my romantic relationship with Swamiji would continue. I expected him to be fonder of me now since I had done such a dreadful thing for his sake. But Swamiji did not want to hear any details of what I had experienced. When I began to talk about the long night of pain and the blood and horror at the end of it, he screwed his face up in disgust and remarked that he didn't want me to talk about it ever again. He seemed strangely aloof towards me but I soon discovered he was even more aloof with Saraswati.

Even though I was physically exhausted and at first had to deal with breasts that swelled and throbbed with unwanted milk (something I was not prepared for and had not even thought of), it was a relief to be back home. Within a few weeks, the abortion seemed truly to be an event of the past as I somehow managed to block any memory of it out of my conscious mind. I was slightly mystified as to why I was so calm and detached about what I had done. It was over a month before I gradually got my strength back and was able to go for short walks.

To my dismay, Swamiji had dropped his beloved Krishna role and was either the detached sage or the angry Rudra destroyer. I was seldom called to his room for daily and nightly dalliances; on the rare occasion that I was, things had changed between us. Swamiji no longer teased me or supported my fantasy about being Radha, his most beloved. He now said our *sangams*, were for him, like washing his teeth. I no longer felt my energy changing or my face becoming softer after we had been together. But any attention was better than none as I waited to re-enter my lost paradise.

Swamiji was now ultra-strict with Saraswati. I kept hoping she would run away and never come back. I could not yet forgive her for abandoning me in Delhi. Evidently Swamiji had been furious at her for coming back early and from that time his relationship with her had also changed. I noticed her face was changing. She began to look like a witch rather than Parvati, the consort of Shiva. Her face was becoming elongated and drawn and her eyes more sunken in their sockets. Her skin broke out into weeping pimples and small abscesses. Her eyes were no longer clear blue and shining. Yellow spots had begun to form, bridging the pupil and the whites of her eyes, which now had a look of haunted fear shadowing them. She often wore robes that had large creamy stains below the curve of her large protruding buttocks; I suspected these were seminal stains that she deliberately had not washed out so as to make me jealous. She often locked herself in her room and would not come out for hours at a time. Swamiji began to call her a witch. I could feel myself gloating uncontrollably when she received her lessons. The veranda door was now bolted from the outside and locked by one of the boys at nighttime. I slept in the Shakti Kutir.

During my first week back, Saraswati and I had had several heated exchanges that resulted in us attacking each other, yanking at each other's hair and biting into each other's arms. I couldn't believe what had erupted between us and also couldn't believe that Swamiji ignored these outbursts. I decided to keep right away from her and ignore her as much as possible.

I began to realise I was no longer Archana. Nor did I feel like the Mary I used to be. A completely foreign personality seemed to be overtaking me. Even though I tried to be in control of my emotions and tried to be peaceful and servile, there were times when anger and hatred overcame me. I would question and argue with Swamiji and seldom cried any more. Residents annoyed me whenever they showed any obedience or loyalty to Swamiji and I found myself gloating whenever anyone ran away or reacted against Swamiji. Swamiji said my 'demon' self was coming out. Buried for years, perhaps lifetimes, perhaps built from memories of past abuse. Perhaps it was punishment, bad *karma*, for having the abortion.

These intense feelings of hate and anger that were being aroused in me seemed to wind up from the pit of my stomach. It was as if the energy from these emotions rose up to my face and settled on the right-hand side. There would be a terrible tightness there and sometimes when I glanced in the mirror I was horrified to see three vertical lines, furrows, appearing above my right eyebrow. I sometimes expected to see horns sticking up out of my head and my upper eye-teeth elongated and hanging over my bottom lip. I would feel a peculiar sensation in these two teeth and I'd sense them growing and protruding, though they never did. I was horrified at these changes.

Whereas previously when I had been the centre of Swamiji's attentions, my face felt like liquid satin, now I felt like plated steel. Swamiji's new name for me became Ardhana, a demonic *asura*. As I had never felt such intense feelings before and I had no idea what to do with them, I tried in vain to push them down again. I accepted Swamiji's explanation that some demonic spirit was overcoming me.

I did not feel this way all the time. I'd feel like it when Swamiji was in one of his Rudra moods and giving me in particular one of his lessons. He began to send me to a small *kutir* on the far side of the property, which was seldom used except as a cooling off station. I was given a new *mantra* to chant continuously; a *mantra* for Mother Goddess Durga — the terrible form Shakti assumes when she goes into battle to combat evil and demonic forces. She is often depicted as riding a tiger and holding various weapons in her ten hands. Her rage and fury serve to fight evil in the world. It never occurred to me that this sort of energy that I was feeling was in fact healthy, a natural outrage at the evil that was Swamiji and his hypocrisy. Instead I fought against it trying to push it down.

The Serpent Rising

On one cold winter morning Swamiji ordered me to go to the far-side *kutir* because he said he could sense the rising of Ardhana. He and the other aspirants all went into the veranda where they sat around the warm *barossi* fire to have *satsang*. The curtains were pulled tightly across now and fastened securely with clothes pegs so as to ward off the cold and the winds that blew up through the valley. But I did not go over to the *kutir*. Instead I lurked around the end of the building straining to try and listen to what they were talking about. I couldn't hear a thing but then they began laughing loudly. I presumed they were laughing at me, so I grabbed the long seven-foot spear that was resting at the end of the building and which we used for protection against wild monkeys and charged through the gap in the curtain.

Swamiji was sitting up near the *puja* place with his back to it and everyone else was sitting in a semi-circle around him. Swamiji smiled impishly when he saw me but the others looked horrified. Michel's curling lips and the glint in his brown eyes betrayed a smugness. I grinned and began to jump around as if I was doing a Maori haka. I hissed and growled and began to thrust the spear in the direction of Swamiji. Strangely enough I could sense a part of me detached and watching these strange antics of mine but at the same time I felt taken over by fury and strong emotion.

Swamiji laughed, 'Your friend visiting you? She's come to pay us a visit?' I felt even angrier. I snarled and blurted out, 'You're a murderer, Swamiji. You killed my baby. You're a sex maniac.' I was shocked to hear these words rushing out of my mouth. I couldn't believe I had actually betrayed Swamiji and our secret. Dropping the spear, I turned and ran out as fast as I could. Swamiji's voice was screeching, 'Go, get her. She's gone too far this time. This time she needs a real lesson.' I thought I was going to be killed for what I had said. Nobody had ever said anything like this to Swamiji or challenged him in this way, not even Mariana.

I had a head start and within minutes had reached the guava garden and was tearing through the thick undergrowth, leaping up and down the undulating path to the far-side *kutir*. On reaching there I darted inside, slammed the door shut and bolted it. I then rushed to the windows closed the shutters and bolted these as well. I sat in the corner of that dark and empty room, panting breathlessly and shivering from the cold, waiting for the boys and Swamiji to come. Perhaps they would break down the door? I was terrified. But nobody came.

I curled up on the floor and lay there for most of the day. I began to remember the terrifying dreams I had had as a young girl about the cannas who molested me. I felt like one of them now. But none of it made any sense. Crouched up in a foetal position I clutched my head and wished that the heat and energy there would disperse. I felt as if it was suffocating me. Sometimes I lapsed into sleep that was neither refreshing nor revealing. This made me feel sluggish, death-like. I just wanted to die.

Towards sunset, I heard Swamiji speaking softly on the other side of the door, 'Has she gone yet?' I opened the door and fell down at his feet. 'I can't take much more of this, Swamiji. Please help me. What's happening to me?' He patted me on the head. 'It's just your past catching up with you. Deep deep *samskaras* from many past lives. Just have faith in Durga Devi. She will help you.' When Swamiji spoke like this I felt relieved and expected that this phase of my life would soon pass. Swamiji said nothing about what I had blurted out that morning. I still couldn't believe why the boys refused to believe that Swamiji slept with us. They also wouldn't believe the number of abortions that had resulted from the raising of energy in the ashram.

Months passed and still Ardhana persisted. During the cold winter months she grew in fury. I spent most of my time curled up in my sleeping bag in the far-side *kutir*, as Swamiji did not want me near him. The bitter biting cold crept under the door and through the cracks in the windows. I felt too lethargic to drag myself up and go for invigorating walks, in the jungle or down to Ganga, to warm myself up. The new *sadhana* and *mantra* for Durga appeared to be making the situation worse. I became more and more depressed and began to wonder whether this *sadhana* would ever work. I wondered whether psychotherapy would help instead. But Swamiji did not believe in such practices and claimed they were mere emotional indulgence. He reminded me that the yogic way was to contemplate the good, the divine, and then the evil inside would gradually transmute into purity. I wanted to believe him. I wanted to believe that these intense demonic energies were actually repressed emotions finally rising and being released, and that deep purification was taking place. It would soon be over and I would be Archana again.

Nevertheless, there were times when I began to wonder whether this was a natural consequence of living in this environment, a reaction to the irrationality and cruel teachings and the madness of Swamiji. Perhaps Swamiji was the madman, the demon possessed. I desperately hoped this was not the case because it would mean that if I had any sense I should leave this place before I went completely insane or committed a truly violent or destructive act.

My faith in Swamiji was lessening. The abortion had marked the beginning of the end. The memory and power of the Third of March was seeping away.

Chapter 10

Letting Go

Two years after that fateful night when all my questions seemed to be answered and almost one year after the abortion, another startling and unexpected thing happened.

One afternoon Swamiji called me into his room and said I should prepare myself as that night he was going to give me another cosmic experience like the Third of March. He thought this might clear out some of my bad *karma* and get rid of Ardhana so Archana could return. A deep sense of relief came over me as this meant that the torment of the past year would soon be over.

And so after supper, when most of the other residents were making preparations to go to bed, I walked up to Swamiji's upstairs bedroom. He was lying down on his cot, gazing up at the ceiling. On seeing me, he lifted his head and shouted, 'Go away, leave me alone. Can't you see I'm meditating?' My heart sank. I told him I wasn't going to leave until he gave me what he promised. I sat down defiantly beside his bed.

Suddenly, Swamiji leapt off the cot and pushed me over. He shouted out to Saraswati, who was downstairs meditating, to come quickly and help him. By the time she reached us, Swamiji was sitting firmly on my chest with his hands tightly gripped around my throat, so tight that I could make no sound except a sort of wet gurgling. His body was so strong I could only twist beneath him. Saraswati leant over me and began slapping me around the face. She yelled, 'How dare you do this to Swamiji. How could you have betrayed him? What's wrong with you?' Then Swamiji began to bang my head on the floor up and down on the concrete floor and seethed, 'And that's for telling Deborah all those things on the train. And that's for telling the boys about the abortion. I've got to get this evil spirit out of you.'

Perhaps he was right. Was he beating Ardhana out of me? But as I lay there it was getting so difficult to breathe that I expected to die.

Suddenly he let go his grip, gave me a few sharp slaps around my face and got up. He fell back on his cot, gasping, 'Saraswati, Saraswati, help. I'm leaving my body. It's time to go home. She's trying to destroy me.'

Saraswati got up, kicked me several times and rushed over to Swamiji. Lying there I found it difficult to breath. The air in the room seemed thick, as if the oxygen was being sucked out of it. Was he really going?

I crawled out of the room, found my way down the stairs to the corner of the veranda and sat huddled there for the rest of the night. The sound of Swamiji's voice reminded me that he was still there. He had not gone after all. It was probably one of his games. My entire body ached and throbbed, especially my head. Blood trickled down into my mouth.

I sat there and stared at the black Himalayan

night until it turned grey and the first light dawned. Only then I did I walk back to the Shakti Kutir to bathe. In the mirror I noticed black bruising and swelling all over my face as well as deep cuts, caked with dried blood, at the corner of my lips. After I had changed clothes, I grabbed a shoulder bag, draped a shawl up over my head to cover my forehead and most of my face and walked around to the kitchen. Swamiji was already there, supervising Jorgen and a new boy light the fire. He was unconcerned at the sight of me and told the boys I had fallen down the steps of the veranda. I said nothing and walked off down the path towards the downside gate. When I reached the bottom I curled up on the grass and lay there for hours waiting for the gate to be opened for visiting time.

When Jorgen finally came down to open the gate, he ignored me and walked down the path to Swargashram, whistling as he went.

It took me about an hour to slowly walk up towards the Laxman Jhula Bridge and on reaching the other side I walked up the side of the river northwards until I found a series of caves that Saraswati had once described to me. I spent the next few days in one of the caves, eating nothing but occasionally drinking Ganga water. My heart was heavy with guilt. I realised I had probably deserved the beating because of all my betrayals of Swamiji first with Deborah and Joe and then my outbursts in the ashram. I had told others 'our secret' (our sacred sex) and also dared to mention the abortion. But I had no idea how to break out of this cycle I seemed trapped in. The more miserable and negative I was, the harsher Swamiji was to me. Perhaps I needed a break away from the ashram.

On returning, I found Swamiji in a dreadful mood. It lasted for weeks. Now he was angry with everyone, so we kept out of his way as much as possible. Saraswati copped most of his anger because she was the only one he would allow to serve him. Finally during the rainy season, Saraswati ran away taking most of her possessions. Swamiji later discovered that in the days prior to her departure she must have stolen his keys to open his safe, as her passport and money were not there. Swamiji was not upset to find her gone. He said, 'I wish you all would leave me now. I don't want to teach Westerners anymore. I just want to be alone, in the bliss of my real nature. Westerners destroy me and take away my purity. I think my teaching time is coming to an end.'

A few months passed and time began to stretch out. A part of me no longer wanted to stay as I had begun to lose faith in Swamiji, but another part was trapped, still holding on in the hope that things would change back to the way they had been in the past. I would be Swamiji's heart again and the centre of his attention. Only the memory of the Third of March sustained me and comforted me, reminding me that I was creating all of this. In my divine creation, Swamiji didn't even exist. There was only love.

Then, about eighteen months after the abortion, what I had most dreaded came to pass. Swamiji snared a new consort. Even though other girls had come and stayed at the ashram during the past year and I suspected that they sometimes shared his bed, his relationship with them was cool and detached.

But one afternoon during the summer heat when things seemed to fade and merge together and we spent more time reading and sleeping, a girl walked slowly up the ashram path. She was bare-footed, wore a white sari, and carried a *sitar*. At first sight of her, I sensed what she would become.

The newcomer was an American from San Francisco who had been studying music with a well-known *veena* master higher up in the mountains in a temple of profound religious significance for Hindus. She was of striking beauty: the skin on her face was almost flawless, her features delicately moulded and her eyes sparkling and almond shaped. She looked slightly overweight by Western standards but Indians typically view excess fat as a sign of beauty. She smiled and laughed a lot and during that first *satsang* she sang devotional songs to Swamiji while playing on her sitar. I noticed Swamiji changing, mellowing, as he flirted playfully with her.

When Swamiji asked her to come and live here, her round face lit up with a full smile. She clasped her hands in joy. She leant over and rested her head on his feet as I looked on in horror. Towards evening she left to catch a bus up to the mountain temple in order to collect her possessions and to say goodbye to her music teacher. Evidently she had been just passing through Rishikesh on her way back from Delhi where she had been to arrange a visa extension. My only consolation was that if she came and stayed here she would leave as soon as she realised that Swamiji's moods changed dramatically. He wasn't just Krishna! This girl looked as if she lacked the strength that Saraswati and I both had. I even entertained the unlikely possibility that her music teacher might try and seduce her and entice her to stay on with him. I at least hoped her visa extension would not be granted so she would have to leave India soon.

But she returned. Swamiji immediately gave her a new name, Padma, which means lotus. He explained that her heart was open like a lotus. That first night she was invited to sleep in the main building and I was sent back to the Shakti Kutir.

I could not sleep. For most of the night I kept creeping up to Swamiji's window to try and hear what was going on inside. There was a candle lit in his room and I could smell his favourite incense. At times I heard faint murmurings or Padma giggling but I heard no sighs, groans or words that I could understand. I kept returning to sit on the hard cot near the tanks of frogs and slime to wallow in self-pity and jealousy. My lotus flowers were no longer in bloom. I burnt some of the poems I had written for Swamiji. I contemplated burning down the ashram or even killing Swamiji.

Early in the morning, before the sun had risen, I packed a few things into a cloth shoulder bag and walked quickly around the boundary of the ashram. I climbed a tree near the corner *kutir* and swung myself over to the back path. I hoped that when Swamiji discovered that I had left he would be full of remorse for the way he had treated me and would send someone to track me down. But this time Swamiji's attention was directed elsewhere.

First I travelled down to the ashram of the Hare Krishnas in Vrindaban. There, wide-eyed, prancing devotees were convinced Lord Krishna himself had sent me so as I could be saved from that rascal Himalayan yogi. They said I was not the first who had sought refuge there but they would not give me any names though I suspected that Saraswati had gone there from time to time because some of the songs she used to sing around the ashram were specifically Hare Krishna ones. Sex was forbidden in this sect until after marriage and then it was only a monthly affair solely for the purposes of procreation and only performed after elaborate and intricate purification rituals. I was given a *mala* bag and beads and instructed to chant rounds and rounds of the Hare Krishna *mahamantra* (great *mantra*) from morning to dusk. But after a fortnight, I slipped through the gates early one morning and caught the first bus out of Vrindaban. The previous evening I had been informed that Krishna was going to bless me with a divine marriage and that a partner had already been selected for me!

With memories of the exquisite stillness and silence experienced in the Vipassana course several years ago, I went back and did two more courses consecutively. Once again I sat for hours and days and tried to watch my breath entering and leaving my nostrils. Once again I sat and watched the changing sensations on the surface of and inside my body. This time it was so much easier. I was able to focus on much subtler sensations, until it was as if my body was a changing river of vibrations and there would arise a profound feeling of relaxation both in my mind and my body. I drank in the quiet and the stillness.

As had happened in the first course, cramps and gripping sensations sometimes spread through my head and around my throat but this time not nearly as frequently or as severe. Previously I had concluded that Swamiji was tuning into my thoughts and trying to lure me back but now I tried to convince myself that these disturbances were not connected with Swamiji. Rather they were just mental blockages coming to the surface from my unconscious mind; mental impressions I had buried and suppressed from reactions to this lifetime and countless past lives. Hadn't I experienced on the Third of March that the mind creates the world? Did this mind of mine even create Swamiji? Hadn't I been shown that the true reality is when the mind ceases to project and hence there is stillness, 'enlightenment'?

Evidently the Buddha also claimed that by introspection and self-observation one could come to know the entire universe, its origins and the way leading to stillness. The goal of Buddhism is the individual's cessation of this mind-created universe by stilling the mind and purifying it of reactive tendencies.

But there was one very big doubt that kept disturbing me for I was not convinced that what I was experiencing during all these courses was in fact my past releasing. What if it wasn't? What if I was actually creating more blockages by all this sitting? How does one know that these sensations and mental disturbances are connected at all, in any way, to the unconscious mind? What if these sensations had nothing to do with the past at all?

Wasn't there a possibility that at times, during all this prolonged sitting, my mind was being interfered with by the spirit Swamiji had called Ardhana? Couldn't other spirits and forces around me attack me especially when my mind was still and calm? Were we not opening ourselves up psychically and yet not protecting ourselves?

But such possession or psychic interference is not considered in the Vipassana way because all reactions are seen as one's own and hence the only solution is to confront these so-called mental knots by one's own efforts without the help of any other person or God.

I was in the same impasse as before. For there seemed to be something missing in these teachings even though in part they agreed with some of my experiences on the Third of March. But what was the origin of those experiences? Surely it was God? I still believed that God was a powerful force, an almighty Being who can intervene in miraculous ways in the lives of believers. I still believed that gurus could inject the power and the love of God into devotees and transform their lives.

Alas, Vipassana was not able to cure me of my need or addiction to gurus. During the next year I travelled thousands of miles across India's endless plains and up and down Himalayan mountains and valleys to visit numerous swamis and yogis in their temples, ashrams or caves. Away from Swamiji, it was easier to love him and blame myself for not being worthy of him. I was determined to change myself so as I could be Archana in Swamiji's divine creation. I tried to believe that all my character changes since coming to India were in fact purifications. All jealousy, anger, hatred were impurities coming to the surface from my unconscious mind. Surely one day I would be free of Ardhana. Surely a time would come when I would no longer resist the Cosmic flow that is manifest in God's anointed ones. My wretched monkey mind would be absorbed into the divine.

India's sweltering summers came and went. The relentless rains of the rainy seasons rose and fell. Wild winds blew through the mountain valleys after the cold winter months, bringing layer upon layer of dust. In the crowded cities Western drug addicts pestered me for rupees whilst young Indian children in tattered clothes, with large brown eyes and runny noses, chased me for *paisa*. Indian men prodded me as if I was a lump of play-dough.

Sometimes I slept in abandoned caves on the banks of rivers on concrete benches on the sides of pilgrim paths. When I stayed at ashrams, I was given a bare room and simpler meals in exchange for servile obedience and small chores, usually cleaning or sweeping. I wandered around India without fear of things on the physical or material level. I believed that God was taking care of me. It mattered little that my worldly possessions were few, that my feet were usually bare. My clothes were a simple white cotton sari, my bedding a straw mat and a single blanket. Hunger never bothered me because I knew that human beings can and have survived weeks without food.

However this is not to say other things did not bother me. At most of the ashrams where I sought refuge, strange pantomimes were being enacted; they were masquerades for harems. Gurus high in the Himalayas and down on the plains preached but did not practise celibacy and restraint of the senses. Elderly swamis lunged at my breasts behind closed doors. Younger swamis invited me for sessions of special *kundalini* raising. I resisted these advances, not that I was wary of reaching the sublime in the *tantric* way but because Swamiji had said he would curse me if I slept with another man. Almost everywhere I went I heard gossip of so-called enlightened or holy men seducing female disciples, usually Westerners. I also learnt that it is not at all uncommon for Western girls to have abortions in Indian hospitals. Usually there is an element of truth in even the most distorted and malicious gossip, but I still concluded that India's god-men were compassionate ego-less beings who merely wanted to raise the *kundalini* of world-weary females in order to erase some of their bad *karma*. When I was in a negative state of mind, however, I wondered whether they were hypocrites and obsessed with sex after being repressed for so long. Whenever I shared my doubts to other Western devotees I was quickly reassured by them that I was not in a position to judge. The level these gurus were operating at was at the level of Truth where there was no morality and one transcends good and evil.

Yet I never heard the slightest gossip of holy Mothers seducing their female or male disciples. The few god-women that I did visit were obese and spent a lot of time eating. But I was told that these gurus were not attached to their food but were working off the *karma* of their devotees.

I wrote the occasional letter to Swamiji telling him how wonderful I was feeling and how much *sadhana* I was doing in other ashrams. Letters, presumably written by Padma (as they were adorned with drawings of pink lotuses) would reach me in various places via poste restante, beseeching me to journey from ocean to source to share again in Swamiji's divine *lila*, his creation of divine love. Swamiji awaited Archana's speedy return, to her real home. The past had been forgotten, the letters said.

When I finally did return, the same dramas were going on. People were still coming and going and running away. Swamiji had had no contact with Saraswati since she had left. Angus was now married with two children and living in Ireland. Jorgen was engaged to be married and had settled in Norway. Michel was still unsettled, roaming around the world returning to the ashram whenever he couldn't cope any more. There were mostly new faces living with Swamiji now.

Padma was still there, though as I had expected she had changed. She had lost her sweetness and did not smile so much. She often chewed on her nails and picked at the pimples bursting out on her chin. Madness erupting. As I watched her face distorting into strange expressions, weird grimaces and glowering, I sensed that her time was ending.

Swamiji was often angry with her but still invited her to receive his yoga energy in the untraditional but increasingly popular way. I wasn't surprised to discover that she had had an abortion five months previously.

Now Swamiji was becoming even more materialistic. The office and cloth room were full of paraphernalia that he had requested from disciples returning from overseas. His collection of tape recorders, radios and watches had grown considerably, plus other objects he was collecting and hoarding. He was even talking about going on world trips to see the cinema of the world and to rescue former disciples.

After a few days I felt tight and contracted again. One evening I burst into Swamiji's room, which he had mistakenly forgotten to lock. I hoped to catch them at it. But they weren't. Padma was lying outstretched on the cot with her clothes on. Swamiji had his arm around her. They both grinned at me when I burst in.

Swamiji said I should return to the West. Wasn't

it time I had my own place, got my own house, lived a life of my own. My cycle had finished a long time ago.

I snarled, 'Why are you so hopeless in bed, Swamiji? You are just like a dog'. He shouted at me to get out and leave in the morning. He said he never wanted to see me again.

I should not have come back. My time had truly passed. I went and sat on the roof of the Kriya Room and stayed up all night. When the morning came, I went and packed my things, slung my backpack over my shoulder and walked briskly past the main building, not pausing to look back. I glanced over at the kitchen and noticed the other residents huddled together waiting for their morning *chai*. I detected looks of smug satisfaction on their faces as if they were glad to see the last of me and because the leaving of anyone made them feel that only they were strong enough to stay.

But it was I who felt triumphant. For the last time I walked down that snaking path. Even though I felt a bitterness in my heart, I also felt a strange detachment. Perhaps that was the only way I could finally leave, extricate myself from Swamiji's clutches.

For the last time I passed through the lotus-spiked gates and walked along the dusty track to the hanging bridge. All the way I kept my eyes focused sharply ahead of me and ignored my surroundings. For once Ganga failed to move me. When I reached the other side of the river I caught a taxi to Hardwar.

Sitting in the back seat of the careering taxi, I felt a strength inside of me, a determination that I had not had before. I vowed to myself that never again would I be dependent on anyone else's energy field, whether guru or teacher. I would wean myself from the drug of Eastern mysticism and the power of those who say they have arrived. I would learn to live without the ecstasy, the bliss and the peace that can be found in temples and ashram and at the feet of those who call themselves *avatars*, Bhagwans, yogis.

I went to the burning ghats at Hardwar while I waited for the train to Delhi. For many hours I sat there watching at a distance as orange flames rose. Even from where I sat the faint smells of roasting flesh drifted up. Black stick-like bones that were once limbs snapped out of the orange fire making loud gunshot noises as if this was their last act of defiance. One black arm refused to crumble into the flame and remained outstretched reaching upwards. Those gathered around a pyre did not seem distraught. They chatted to each other while they stoked the flames, threw *ghee* and fresh flowers on the disappearing body or sang farewell prayers for a safe journey into the next world, and the next incarnation.

Far better this way than the slow disintegration of those who passed fully clothed in my river nearby because their loved ones had no money for wood. I had heard that decomposed corpses occasionally drift in amongst the locals going about their routines of washing clothes, bathing and even drinking the water. The locals would be unperturbed about this, and no doubt just push the corpses away with sticks. Death here in India is very much at home, a part of life, not hidden away and sanitised as it is in the West.

Standing up I looked up the river to the mountains in the distance, a place where a boy-yogi lives. 'How I have loved that strange person and how I have feared him. What torment and what ecstasy have ripped through my life since my first meeting with him.'

I turned away and walked slowly to the station where I could rest for the remainder of the day and be close to a toilet. My physical body was in a wretched state. Intestinal parasites of various strains had taken up residence in my gut over a year before and were long resistant to courses of Flagyl. In addition, large abscesses that were excruciatingly painful had been breaking out in various places on my body over the past few weeks.

While in Delhi making arrangements for my flight home, an abscess the size of a bread and butter plate spread over my right buttock. It seemed to me that India was giving me one final slap. This monstrous abscess was pierced and gouged without a local anaesthetic in an overcrowded hospital in Old Delhi where even the corridors housed very sick patients, some of whom lay on the floor with drips in their arms. When the procedure was complete, I was ordered to leave the hospital immediately to make room for another patient. Somehow I managed to drag myself along the floor and out onto the footpath to call for a rickshaw.

I postponed my flight for a further two weeks, as I wanted to at least be able to walk off the plane in Auckland with some dignity. I was horrified to discover that the hole that had been gouged in my buttock was over one inch in diameter and deep enough for my entire forefinger to slip inside. But the wound healed miraculously within days after it was padded with gauze soaked in a solution of calendula, a homeopathic remedy that I purchased from a roadside pedlar near my hotel.

I wrote to my parents saying they would not have to worry about me any more as I was finally coming home for good. I apologised for any heartache my Eastern explorations had caused over the years. But my mother, being a nurse, had been mostly concerned about my physical health in India. She had written to me regularly but never questioned what I was doing or tried to talk me into returning. Perhaps if she had objected to what I was doing, I might have ceased communicating altogether. My Indian dream was something I had to work out in my own time, by myself. Now I felt an enormous gratitude to my parents for their tolerance and support and felt ashamed for the way I had judged and criticised them in the past.

And so the night came when I was to leave this country I had called Mother Bharat, this country I had both adored and hated. As the rickshaw bumped its way to the airport, I clung to my bags for fear that at the next bump they would be thrown out. Misty shadows flitted past, tall trees and bushes seemed to jump out at me. Dogs' howls pierced the darkness.

Suddenly the driver slammed on the brakes of the rusted rattling vehicle. We spun around on the gravel creating a cloud of dust. The driver leapt out. I stooped and slid across the torn seat-cover taking care not to hit my head on the rail overhead as I had done so many times in these past few years. The driver's hands began clutching and fumbling at the fly buttons of his drab grease-stained khaki trousers that were sizes too big for him. He was about two metres away from me. My first thought was that he wanted to urinate. But then he lunged at me. 'Want some corruption, memsahib?' he stammered nervously. I almost laughed. Instead I threw back my head and let out a shattering scream. I felt the sounds coming up from the pit of my stomach, blasting outwards. In a wild rage I charged forward and threw my hands around his sweaty neck. He had no shirt on. A cheap *mala* with a trinket of Hanuman the monkey god hung over his hairless chest. I felt like ripping the beads off him. 'You take me to the airport or I'll kill you,' I screeched.

His body began to tremble and a look of terror came over him. He nodded his head from side to side. I let go my grip and clambered back into the rickshaw. I breathed deeply. The driver leapt back into the front seat leaving his trousers gaping at the front. I clambered back in, shaken by my anger but also relieved that I was no longer the little mouse I once had been.

The rest of the journey passed without incident. When we finally arrived and I had scrambled out dragging all my luggage after me, the driver took off at great speed without so much as a glance in my direction or any mention of *paisa* for the fare.

I felt sick. Is this how you are going to farewell me, Mother India, with a sore bottom and a sex-starved rickshaw driver? I am so tired. I just want out. I want to go home and rest. I don't want your heaven any more because I can't bear the hell that goes with it. I am not strong enough for your God. Now I just want to be one of those ordinary people of the world that your gurus seem to despise so much.

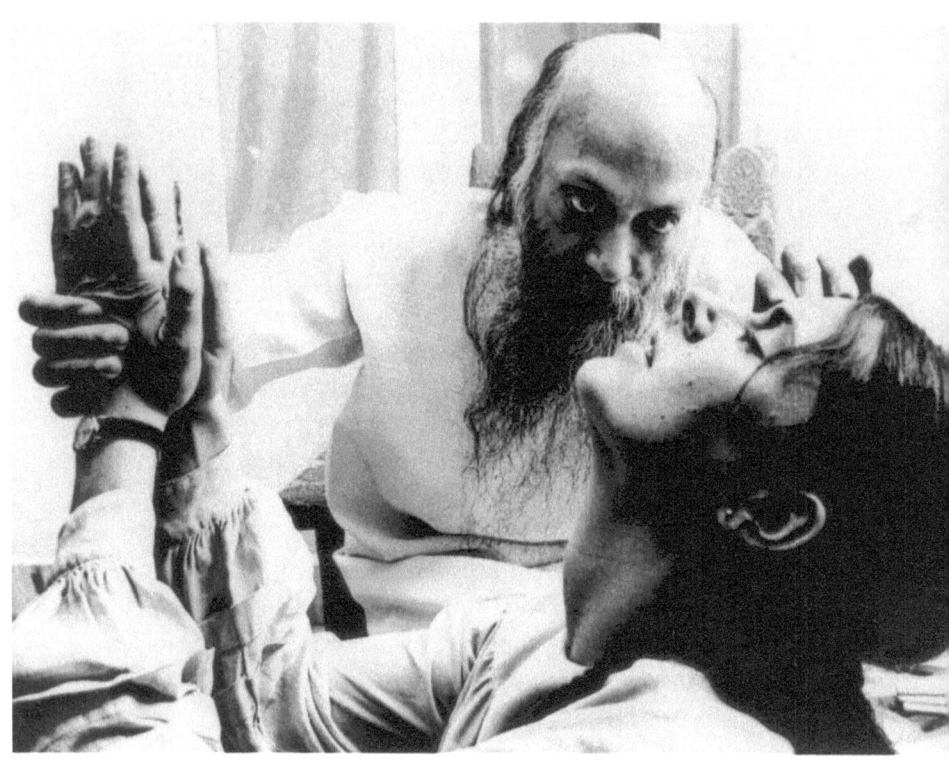

Mary Garden having an 'Energy Darshan' with Rajneesh (Osho), Poona, India, November 1979

Epilogue

Coming Home

I retreated back into worldly life to find I had been given an unexpected parting gift from India — hepatitis. Perhaps I had caught it from the scalpel that had been plunged into my swollen, abscessed buttock. For the first few months in New Zealand I felt like an alien from another planet, and indeed was treated as such as I was still wafting around in white robes, *mala* beads and a spaced-out look in my eyes. However this was an opportunity to rest and recover my physical health and to indulge in warm baths and soft beds.

I would like to be able to say that this was the end of my exotic story, that I settled back into 'normal Western life' and this was the end of my addiction to gurus. But it wasn't. It was the end, however, of my devotion to Swamiji even though it was many years before I resolved my ambivalence over who and what he was. I found it heart-wrenching to be away from India in spite of everything and New Zealand did not feel like home at all.

Then I met up with some Rajneesh devotees in Auckland and began doing their 'strange' meditations and attending their parties. They were nothing like devotees of other gurus and were doing something that no other guru was incorporating into his or her teaching: psychotherapy. The latter was to change my life for the better (in a way that my spiritual trips never had) and, ironically enough, help me overcome my need for gurus, including Rajneesh himself.

I travelled to Brisbane in Australia and spent six months teaching before returning to India, to the Rajneesh Ashram in Poona. I became a *sannyasin* and received a new name Ma Prem Sagara, meaning ocean of love. Rajneesh, or Bhagwan as we called him, was a magnet for Western seekers because of his combination of psychotherapy and New Age practices with Eastern techniques. Therapists who had previously been well known and respected in their home countries had come to Poona and now led therapy groups such as Encounter, Primal, Gestalt, and Reichian.

This therapy was a time of healing for me. It was radically different from anything I had ever done before. As well as reliving the trauma of the abortion, healing took place (I believe) from deeper psychological wounds from childhood, which yoga and meditation had failed to heal. In padded cell-like subterranean rooms with groups of up to twenty people I screamed, yelled, laughed, cowered, pushed and hugged my way out of the madness of repressed emotions.

At last, for the first time in my life, I was no longer at war with my feelings. I had been taught by my parents, teachers, and then Hindu gurus, that emotions and feelings are bad — especially anger but also fear. Now here at Poona I was finally given permission to not only feel but also express what I felt. It was a liberating time for me. That year was the happiest I was ever to have in India — the happiest in my life up to that point. I also laughed and smiled more and would burst into song as I rode my old rental pushbike around the streets of Poona. I began to enjoy dancing with abandon during the dynamic and *kundalini* meditations.

Swamiji was not completely out of my mind, however. Since leaving him I had been wary of men and avoided relating closely with them. At the second of three interviews I was to have with Rajneesh he instructed me to return to the Himalayan Hill as I needed to learn to love all the flowers in the flower garden, not just the rose which, he added, has thorns. He also spoke about the hypocrisy of the Indian swamis and gurus who preach but don't practise celibacy. He insisted that if I went back there one more time, I would see things differently and be finally able to let go of this yogi.

And so I went back once more. Things were very different for me this time. It was as if I had outgrown the ashram or found something better to replace it. I no longer felt love for Swamiji or any need to worship him; he was no longer my guru. It was also an unusually quiet time in the ashram and his mind was seldom present — it was away on other disciples. Rajneesh was right. I did see Swamiji in a different light. After a few weeks I missed Poona, the openness and the freedom there. Swamiji noticed that Ardhana had disappeared and said I had 'matured'. But he said I was not ready for his pure teachings and obviously needed to spend time in the gutter with Rajneesh and all those pseudo-swamis. Some time though, in the future, he claimed, I would return with all the other *gopis* for good. We would all live together in peace, in a state of Superconsciousness, and we would often dance, in bliss, in the Circle.

When I returned to Poona, I assisted American author Bernard Gunther with the compilation of a book for Rajneesh called 'Neo-Tantra'. This was a good time to be in Poona in many respects. It was before the move to Oregon where things went downhill rapidly and various abuses of power hit the world press. As with all groups, being at the periphery (often in ignorance of the dramas being played out close to the guru himself) is usually less damaging. In Poona the majority of us lived outside the ashram, rented apartments and lived (mostly) our own lives. There were excesses and extremes in the underground cells where we did therapy but I survived unscathed, if not strengthened by my experiences there.

Towards the end of the year things in Poona began to turn a corner and gradually become more bizarre. There were several suicides, murders, and rapes for example, and armed guards were posted at the gates. I decided to leave. My mother had sent me a newspaper cutting of the Jim Jones mass suicide at Jonestown and this news freaked me out. For some reason I believed a similar tragedy could happen with the Bhagwan. It was time to get out and I decided to return to Brisbane, Australia and finally settle down.

This semi-tropical city reminded me of some of the beautiful things of India. There always seemed to be doves calling to each other, there was a long river snaking through its centre, streets were lined with jacaranda trees and most gardens sported jasmine and frangipani. There were also the warm sultry summers to slow me down.

I wanted no more contact with Swamiji again but Michel managed to track me down three years later. By that time I was married, with an infant son and was expecting a second child. Michel departed for the Himalayan Hills, presumably with a tale that Archana was truly caught in the treacherous ocean of worldly life.

Even though motherhood and marriage provided my life with stability, an anchor previously not experienced, it was a long and slow process to wake up and see Swamiji for what he really was and is: a dangerous and violent megalomaniac. Only then could I fully extract him from my mind and recover from his extraordinary abuse.

At the time of writing Swamiji (Swami Balyogi Premvarni) is still alive and unfortunately still up to his old tricks. His web site describes him as a spiritual guide and Yoga expert: 'The gems of wisdom and love which radiate from his heart deeply uplift the spirits of those who experience the blessings of his presence'. His mission is stated as: 'Awakening Super consciousness in spiritual aspirants'.

Thanks to the Internet, many seekers who have visited the Himalayan Hill have con-tacted me. All have been puzzled, confused and disturbed by what they experienced and all have the same question: is it him or me? Was he 'testing me' or is he downright abusive?

The guru-disciple relationship is probably the most authoritarian in its demand for total surrender and obedience and hence potentially the most destructive of all relationships. And so, far from achieving the freedom and 'enlightenment' that many of us wannabe spiritual pioneers of the 70's went looking for (and indeed were promised), we experienced mental imprisonment and confusion. Those of us who fell for flawed gurus, unwittingly entered a door into a world called derangement, which we regarded as heaven but which in fact was a form of hell. We were seduced by yogis and swamis telling us what we wanted to hear: that we were special and that they were God-incarnate. Our need was our downfall. In the final analysis the authority of the guru is bestowed on him by the disciple!

It is now fifty years since I first set foot in India and felt at last I had come home. From time to time in my now busy life, I look back on those years when my heart was captured and my mind imprisoned and it seems more and more like a strange dream or play in which I once participated. I even have difficulty in recognising myself as the main character.

Yet despite its strangeness, this is also the story of thousands of others who have gone searching for something better, some of whom have still not woken up. I am grateful that I did manage to wake up, escaped, and survived to tell the tale.

Glossary

Almari	Cupboard
Anapana	The first step of Vipassana meditation: the watching of one's natural, normal breath as it enters and leaves the nostrils
Asura	Evil spirit, demon
Arti (or Arati)	(lit. 'light') A religious ritual performed by rotating an oil lamp in a clockwise circle usually around the idol of a saint, a god or goddess or a Shiva *lingam*
Asanas	(lit. 'seat') Yoga postures
Ashram	An abode of a saint or guru and spiritual aspirants
Atman	Individual 'soul'
Avatar	(lit. 'descent') Incarnation of God upon earth
Baksheesh	A charitable offering, alms
Barossi	Portable fireplace on which hot coals are placed
Beedi (or Bidi)	Cheap hand-rolled cigarette wrapped in a leaf
Bhagavad Gita	(lit. 'Song of the Lord') Dialogue in the Mahabharata between the warrior Arjuna and Lord Krishna who encourages him to do his duty in battle reminding him that the souls of those he kills will not die but will reincarnate
Bhagwan	God, Lord (title bestowed on Rajneesh and on many gurus)
Bhajan	Devotional song sung to the accompaniment of musical instruments
Bhakta	Devotee

Bharat	India
Brahmâ	The Creator aspect of God, the first god in the Hindu Trimurti, usually shown with four heads and four hands holding prayer beads and a manuscript
Brahmacharya	(lit. 'religious living') Path to God where sexual abstinence is obligatory
Brahman	The Great Soul, the supreme transcendental reality
Catori	Bowl made of aluminium or stainless steel
Chakras	(lit. 'wheels') Supposed subtle energy centres located in seven regions of the body such as heart and the throat
Chai	Indian tea made with milk, tea-leaves, sugar and spices
Chapatti	Thin, unleavened wheat bread usually round in shape
Charpoi	Rope-strung bed
Choli	Blouse worn under a sari
Cot	Bed with flat wooden base
Darshan	(lit. 'sight') To have *darshan* refers to be in the presence of a guru or saint and receiving a blessing by that mere fact
Devi	Goddess
Dhobi wallah	Washerman
Ducca	Suffering
Durga	Form of the goddess Shakti that is the destroyer of demons
Elaichi	Cardamon (a spice often used in *chai*)
Enlightenment	Liberation from the cycle of reincarnation
Ganesh	The god of knowledge and remover of obstacles; portrayed with an elephant's head, large stomach and four arms
Ganga	Ganges River
Ghee	Clarified butter. Considered holy by Hindus because it comes from the cow. Used in temple lamps etc.
Glass	Sometimes used to refer to a tall thin tumbler without a handle, made from stainless steel or aluminium and used for *chai* or other drinks

Gopi	Cowgirl, love companion of Krishna in Hindu mythology
Grihastha	Householder
Gulab-jamun	Sweetmeat of flour, yoghurt, almonds and sugar
Guna	Energy. Yoga philosophy delineates three *gunas*: *tamasic, rajasic* and *sattwic*. These are used to describe types of food, people or practices
Guru	(lit. 'one who leads a disciple from darkness to light') Spiritual guide
Hanuman	The monkey god; god of power and strength. The greatest devotee of Lord Rama
Hari Om	Greeting
Hatha yoga	Physical postures (*asanas*) performed to control the mind as well as the body
Kali	Goddess of time who destroys everything; aspect of Parvati
Kajal	Black eye makeup applied to the borders of the eyelids
Karma	(lit. 'action' or 'deed') Hindu law of cause and effect that teaches that every thought or word creates an effect reaped in the present or subsequent lifetimes
Karma Yoga	Yoga of action or good deeds; path of selfless service
Khadi	Hand-spun and hand-woven textile of India
Krishna	One of the most popular deities in Hinduism. Considered to be the eight incarnation of Vishnu
Kriyas	Practices to purify the body usually through the use of water
Kudabox	(colloq.) Idiot, fool
Kundalini	(lit. 'serpent power') Hindus believe that this divine power lies like a serpent in the root *chakra*' at the base of the spine. The aim of some yoga practices is to awaken *kundalini* energy and transmute it to higher consciousness

Kunjal Kriya	Rapid drinking and then retching of salty water
Kutir	Cottage
Lassi	Cold whisked drink made of water, yoghurt and sugar
Lila (or Leela)	(lit. 'play' or 'divine sport') The actions of the Supreme Being or a guru
Lingam	The phallic symbol associated with Lord Shiva
Lungi	Sarong-style loin-wrap for male(s)
Mala	108-beaded necklace used like a rosary
Malai	Cream
Mandir	Temple
Mantra	Word of phrase recited repetitively as a sacred formula
Mataji	'Respected Mother'
Maya	Illusion; Hindus regard the physical world as *maya* or illusionary
Namaste	Hindu greeting usually given with clasped hands and a polite bow in recognition of the Universal Self of the other
Mouna	The keeping of silence, not talking
Nauli	Yoga *kriya* involving 'churning' the abdominal column left and right
Neti lota	Brass container with long spout; when filled with warm salty water it used to clean nasal passages
Nirvana	Blissful state associated with achieving 'unity with the divine'
Om (or Aum)	ॐ Considered by Hindus to be the primordial sacred sound of the universe
Paisa	Indian currency
Parabramha	Supreme Godhead; absolute reality
Paramatma	Supreme self
Parvati	Consort of Shiva
Prana	(lit. 'breath') The principle of life moving in the human body
Pranam	Reverent salutation or greeting where the head of body is bowed
Pranayama	Yoga breathing exercises
Puja	Ceremonial worship of gods or a guru

Radha	Most beloved of Krishna's lovers (*gopis*)
Rajasic	Passionate or if applied to food — stimulating or over-spiced
Rama	Incarnation of Lord Vishnu
Ramayana	The great *Sanskrit* epic of the story of how Lord Rama rescued his wife Sita from the clutches of the demon Ravana
Resai	Thin mattress
Rudra	The name for Shiva when he is the god of dissolution or destruction; revered as 'the terrifying one'
Rudraksha	(lit. 'eye of Shiva') Marble-sized reddish brown seeds from the Eleocarpus ganitrus, or blue marble tree. Devotees of Shiva often use them for necklaces or prayer beads
Sadhaka	Spiritual aspirant
Sadhana	A course of spiritual teaching or practices
Sadhu	Hindu ascetic usually with no fixed abode and few possessions
Samadhi	State of 'super consciousness'
Samsara	(lit. 'flow') The cycle or chain of birth, death and rebirth through a series of earthly lives, the phenomenal world
Samskaras	Supposed impressions in the unconscious from reactions (clinging and avoiding) in the present or past lifetimes
Sangam	Confluence
Sannyas	Vows of renunciation
Sannyasin	One who has retired from worldly life to devote himself to spiritual concerns
Sanskrit	The sacred tongue of Hinduism; Indo-European language brought to India during the second millennium BC
Saraswati	Goddess of learning; consort of Brahma
Satsang	A religious meeting for worship or teaching purposes
Sattwic (or Sattva)	Calm, peaceful, pure or if applied to food – easy to digest
Shakti (or Sakti)	Another name for Parvati, Shiva's consort. The manifest energy of the Supreme Power

Shankaracharya	Great Vedanta philosopher who lived in the 8th century AD
Shiva (or Siva)	The third god in the Hindu trimurti; the destroyer
Siddhi	(lit. 'power') Occult power gained through the higher stages of Yoga
Sitar	Seven-stringed instrument played with the fingers
Swami	A term used as a title for a guru or the head of an order
Tamasic	Sluggish, stale or if applied to food — stale, over-ripe
Tantra	Ancient system of using sexual energy to attain spiritual enlightenment
Tapas	The austerity of an ascetic
Thali	Tray
Tiffin tins	Set of metal containers to carry home-cooked foods
Tilak	Mark on forehead made from red powder or paste
Tonga	Two-wheeled taxi carriage usually drawn by a man, sometimes by a horse
Tulsi	Sweet basil
Upanishads	Part of the *Vedas*
Vedanta	Systematic exposition of the *Vedas*
Vedas	The oldest Hindu religious texts
Vedic	From the *Vedas*
Veena	Indian lute
Vibhuti	Sacred ash of Hinduism; made from burnt cow dung
Vishnu	The second god in the Hindu trimurti; the preserver
Yatra	Pilgrimage
Yoga	(lit. 'to yoke') Union of individual self (*atman*) with the Supreme Being: Brahman
Yoga kriyas	Practices to purify the body, usually through the use of water
Yogi	An advanced practitioner of yoga
Yoni	Hindu vaginal symbol; usually represented cupping the Shiva *lingam*

www.ingramcontent.com/pod-product-compliance
Lightning Source LLC
Chambersburg PA
CBHW031239290426
44109CB00012B/362